Using Gravity!

The Power of Standing Zen

Get unshakable balance with the Tripod Method

By Ojiro Matsui

Translated by Remy Castella

BAB JAPAN

Using Gravity! The Power of Standing Zen
Get unshakable balance with the Tripod Method

Author: Ojiro Matsui
Translator: Remy Castella

Published by BAB JAPAN CO.,LTD
30-11 SASAZUKA 1-CHOME, SHIBUYAKU, TOKYO 151-0073 JAPAN
Tel.03-3469-0135 Fax.03-3469-0162
E-mail.shop@bab.co.jp
URL.http://www.bab.co.jp/
http://budojapan.com/
http://webhiden.jp/

Cover Design: Hideyuki Yanaka
Interior Design: Miyoko Sawakawa
Illustrations: Kirara Tsukiyama

Author: Ojiro Matsui

Director of Taikiken Buzen-kai. Born in 1972. He was a former vice-captain of the Waseda Nipponkempo Club, where he won technical awards and other prizes at student championships. After graduation, he practiced mixed martial arts and later began training under Master Michio Shimada of Taiki Shisei Kenpo Kikou-kai. He has since won numerous awards, including winning a Sanda competition, and is currently working to spread Taikiken, mainly in Sapporo. He is also a non-regular contributor to the martial arts magazine 'HIDEN' and regularly interacts with martial arts instructors from various schools.

Translator: Remy Castella

Graduated from the University of Vermont with a Bachelor of Science in Neuroscience and currently works as a freelance translator based in Sapporo. He has practiced various martial arts since childhood, including Brazilian Jiu-Jitsu and Capoeira, and now trains under Master Ojiro Matsui of Taikiken Buzen-kai.

Introduction

Taikiken Buzen-kai
Ojiro Matsui

It's gravity, not muscle strength.

The "power" required in sports and martial arts comes from gravity rather than muscle strength. In other words, it comes from balance and your ability to connect with the ground. Even if the same boxer were to punch with the same speed, distance, and angle, the force of impact would depend greatly on form. Also, what makes someone a hard puncher? Is it their power and speed, or their courage to lunge forward?

Take sumo wrestlers. Their power undoubtedly comes from their weight and muscle strength. But it isn't always the bigger and stronger wrestler that wins. What happens when a smaller wrestler hurls a stronger and heavier opponent?

Punching and pushing have something in common. In both cases, at least three parts of the body are in contact with an external point, including both soles of the feet and another point somewhere on the body (such as the fist or chest). You are exerting force with three external points of contact while maintaining your posture. This is nothing more than an expression of balance.

When I say balance, you might think of the ability to maintain your posture when your footing is unstable, such as when surfing or walking across a tightrope. However, continuing to play while being aggressively pushed around, such as in soccer and other sports, is also an expression of balance. When it comes to maintaining a well-balanced posture and physical structure, muscle strength is a secondary factor—it, by itself, isn't the "power" or "influence over your opponent" that we're after. And, in land-based sports, the type of balance that stabilizes you against external resistance is probably more useful than the type required when your footing is unstable.

The Tripod Method, the subject of this book, is a method for maintaining your balance and converting your body weight into force when you have three external points of contact (both soles of your feet and one more point of contact). This method is based on Ritsuzen, an exercise in traditional martial arts and Qigong, and this ability is innate in everyone—it doesn't have to be learned. All you have to do is become aware of it.

Chapter 1

A Mysterious Power Handed Down in the Martial Arts

Power That Doesn't Come from Muscles

A training method called Ritsuzen has been handed down in Taiki Shisei Kenpo (commonly called Taikiken). We raise our arms in front of our chests as if hugging a ball and just keep standing. **<Figure 1-1>** After a while, you'll feel the elasticity of the ball in your arms and a sensation of being suspended by a string attached to the crown of your head. There's also a sense of being pulled apart in all directions and a resistance as if you were standing underwater. These sensations are sometimes referred to as "sensations of qi." Ritsuzen is an ancient Chinese Qigong exercise that is known as Zhan Zhuang over there. Since it's derived from Qigong, its primary purpose could be considered cultivating qi and promoting physical and mental health.

This "qi" is said to not decline with the body as we age. It's a power that enables old masters to subdue brawny youngsters—one that doesn't come from muscles. It's been passed down through the generations via sensory and abstract language, through direct contact between master and disciple.

There are countless anecdotes of Kenichi Sawai, the founder of Taikiken, and his master, Wang Xiangzhai, blasting away opponents with ease. Michio Shimada, who is Sawai's direct disciple and my master, possesses similar abilities. I've seen him easily overpower opponents numerous times.

It's been over 20 years since my first encounter with Taikiken, and I currently oversee the Taikiken Buzen-kai, which my master has appointed, and train with its members in Sapporo. But, to tell you the

<Figure 1-1> Ritsuzen is known as Zhan Zhuang in Qigong and Chinese martial arts, and it cultivates a tremendous power that transcends muscular strength!

truth, I had no idea how to acquire the power I had witnessed in my master until a few years ago.

I have felt a baffling power when interacting with masters of various schools, not limited to Taikiken. But what was it? Was it all the same? Could it be acquired through practice?

Maybe I would have been stronger if I had spent my 20 years in traditional martial arts on modern training, lifting weights, and hitting sandbags instead. Perhaps my years had gone to waste. I carried such doubts ceaselessly. Was there even such a thing as a power that doesn't decay with age, the power of qi? And could it be mastered?

While I continued my Taikiken training, my worries were endless.

Meeting the Zen Monk

One day, Master Koyou Shigeo of Touzen introduced me to Master Mitsugu Yamamoto of Ryusuiken.

Ryusuiken is an internal martial art based on Zhang-style Tai Chi founded by Master Takeo Narasaki, and Master Yamamoto is its 3rd generation leader. Such a person lived about 10 minutes away from my home in Sapporo. Not wanting to pass up this opportunity, I began practicing with him regularly. I learned a lot from Master Yamamoto. He has trained in various martial arts, including Ryusuiken and Taikiken, and his techniques, from the so-called internal martial arts, were refined through combat. The internal martial arts refer to three styles, Tai Chi, Ba Gua Zhang, and Xing Yi Quan, and they emphasize the mind and qi. I hear this isn't always the best term as it's tinged with an intention to mystify one's style, but I'd like to use it in this book without discriminatory intent.

When I would ask Master Yamamoto about his martial arts background during breaks, the name of a Zen monk kept coming up. Apparently, when he laid his hands on the monk, a powerful blast would send him flying back. Was it even possible to blast people away like that? But the Zen monk's name sounded familiar, so I looked him up. He was indeed the man rumored to be a hidden martial arts master. Many renowned martial artists revered this monk and described his power as extraordinary. Could there really be such a master? If there really was such a master in our time, I had to meet him.

So, I asked Master Yamamoto about the whereabouts of this Zen monk. While he gave me the address, the monk apparently doesn't have a landline, let alone a smartphone. He doesn't have a dojo, either. A letter will have to do. Up until then, I had never written a letter to a stranger. But I couldn't let that hold me back. There was a martial arts master hidden from the world in our modern era.

I wrote my wish to meet and learn martial arts from him. But a month had passed with no reply. I didn't let that stop me. Knowing it was impolite, I decided to intrude anyway. When I looked up the address on Google Maps, the pin dropped deep in the mountains. Would the monk really be there? I had my doubts, but I also had to go.

Determined, I visited the backcountry residence on a hot summer Sunday. Fortunately, the Zen monk was home, so I apologized for my surprise visit and briefly introduced myself. It turns out the monk had read my letter, and he invited me inside. The house, where the monk had been living for several decades, was spotless, as if he'd moved in yesterday. A pristine space with nothing out of place—just like a Zen temple.

The monk was a small, elderly man dressed in a samue, close to 80 years old. He had a tranquil presence, as if he were asleep. While he certainly didn't look like a martial arts master, that made him seem even more like the real deal. An enigma whose depths couldn't be fathomed—that was my first impression of him. In his youth, he had apparently spent a few years walking throughout Hokkaido as a mendicant, and I listened to his many stories as he showed me pictures from that time.

After tuning into his stories for a while, I told the monk that I had come to learn martial arts. "Martial arts hurt people. Such things are unnecessary," the monk replied bluntly. Not able to give up, I pleaded once again.

"There was supposed to be heavy rain today, but we were blessed with clear skies. I also happened to be home. Maybe this was meant to be," the monk said, instructing me to meet him in his yard. A typhoon had caused heavy rains the past few days, and the storm had canceled the flights before mine out of Hokkaido, where I lived. I hadn't noticed when we were sitting in the tatami room, but the monk had apparently injured his leg badly when he was younger, and even putting on his shoes seemed to be a struggle. I remember feeling bad asking him to teach me martial arts and wondering if he would be okay.

In the yard, the Zen monk stood about 50 cm before me. "Push me," he said. I complied. He doesn't budge. I had pulled my punch due to his age. I push him again, this time with more force—and no sign of movement. Maybe I could push him hard, I thought, shoving him with all my strength. Then, for some reason, it was me, not the monk, who flew backward. I didn't understand. Not only could I not push this small elderly man with a bad leg, he had hurled me back. It didn't feel like I pushed something rigid. Instead, it was like bouncing off an elastic ball. I had no idea what had happened. So, I tried again, flying back once more. According to the monk, "Your body just needs to become like an air-filled tire. Wherever you are pushed, make that the ground. Then, your opponent will be going against the ground, not you." It truly did feel like that.

After that, the monk showed me some exercises. The movements were very similar to what we have in Taikiken, and above all, Ritsuzen was at the heart of his martial art. Ritsuzen is also the most important exercise in Taikiken. I couldn't help but feel a special connection. I asked the monk the name of his style. "Don't know."

He learned the art while living in a cave for a few years with an old master, but the master never told him his name or the name of his martial art. But for me, style isn't important. After experiencing the monk's power, I needed to acquire it for myself. And after some pleading, he granted me permission to frequent his home.

Discovering the Rubber Ball Power

When I returned to Sapporo, I repeated the exercises I had learned. While teachings can be totally opposed between different styles, luckily, the monk's movements were very similar to Taikiken. I suspect his martial art draws from the internal martial arts, and it doesn't feel like training it will hinder my martial art. For example, in Taikiken, we move back and forth in a straight line while rotating the arms in front of the body. The monk's teaching, on the other hand, involves walking in a circle with similar arm movements. There's this difference, of either a straight line or circle, but the arm movements, positioning of the waist, and so on, were almost identical.

The Zen monk would also push various parts of my body as I walked, checking if I wobbled. While there wasn't much teaching through words, through this training, I sensed that "making your body like an air-filled tire" and "making wherever you're pushed the ground" were the essence of the monk's teachings.

The power developed through martial arts is referred to as Neigong or Kungfu, and there is something called the "ball-like power," where the body is supposed to become elastic like a ball filled with air. Pushing the monk felt exactly like pushing a ball filled with air—this was probably the power I had felt.

My clues were in the two, three simple exercises I was taught and the sensation I felt when I pushed him. That was all. One night, after a few months of trial and error, I was in deep contemplation while standing alone in Ritsuzen.

In the martial arts, we say that power comes from the legs. Even when throwing a punch, the legs are crucial. The Zen monk also said to make whoever touches you fight the ground.

But the monk had a bad leg, unable even to walk well. He can't be using his legs…

Hmm… Fight the ground? Oh! He *was* using his legs but not *using* them!

This was when a part of the power of Ritsuzen and the martial arts became clear to me.

The monk's power truly wasn't from his muscles. It was a power that the body—nature—inherently possessed. Everyone had this power, and it was something that could be explained physically and reproduced. This wasn't some mysterious power after all. It was a logical power. All I had to do was train to make this power more reproducible. Once I knew how this power worked, I understood that it was the aim of all the monk's exercises. In academia, the knowledge of our predecessors is passed down through writing. In the martial arts, however, realizations are passed down through exercises, and the exercises are the realizations themselves. It became clear that the monk's elusive words, "making your body like a tire," weren't an evasion—they were spot on. While the Zen monk uses "air-filled tire" to describe this power, I would like to express it as the Rubber Ball Power from my own sensations.

Chapter 2

What is the Tripod Method?

Something That Comes Before Form and Muscle Strength

To improve your performance in martial arts and sports, you must incorporate the following in a balanced manner: learning the optimal form for that sport; improving the foundational fitness required for that sport (explosiveness, endurance, etc.); and gaining hands-on experience (through competitions for example).

In the martial arts, you would learn the proper forms for punching, kicking, throwing, and joint locks, and how to use each technique. Additionally, you would incorporate push-ups, bench presses, squats, and running to improve your foundational fitness. Then, with this foundation, you would likely gain practical experience through competitive training.

However, you may have felt that having the "correct" form or excellent fitness doesn't always lead to competitive ability. In fact, the basic forms may even be unusable during competition. For example, you might learn the traditional punches and kicks during basic training but learn a different set of techniques for competition.

The training system above can be represented as Power = Form x Fitness. While the equation for competitive ability is likely Form x Fitness x Practical Know-How, I won't be mentioning competition-specific strategies in this book as I am focusing on "power." Within this framework, if one's competitive ability isn't improving as expected, they'd say, "He's strong, but his punches are too wide" (form issue), "His form is good, but his legs are weak" (fitness issue), "He isn't used to competing" (problem with practical know-how), or even "He lacks the grit to push forward" (mental factors at last). And if they still couldn't figure it out, they'd say, "He just doesn't have it."

This approach divides human movement into small components such as fitness (power, speed, etc.), form, experience, psychology, etc. However, in the complex system that is the human being, the whole isn't always the sum of its parts.

I believe something is missing in such training methods. This "something" is what ties together form and fitness. It could also be called the relationship between form and muscle strength.

For example, take the goal of throwing a heavy (strong) straight punch. In a competition, strong punches are a means. The goal is to win by hitting the right spot and knocking out your opponent. While we shouldn't turn the means into an end, this often happens during practice. And when we analyze things through reason, they take on a nested structure like a Matryoshka doll.

To throw a punch correctly, you must draw your arms in, make a certain shape with your fists, tighten that muscle, etc. Like this, every style has its form. And if two people have the same form, the one with more strength will have a stronger punch—or so the theory would go.

This seems right at first, but two people with the same form, strength, and weight will not necessarily punch with the same force. This is because the human body has over 200 joints and comes in varying shapes, making it impossible for two people to recreate the same form in the first place. In other words, there isn't a universally correct form.

Trying to master the correct form only ever amounts to achieving the "roughly correct" form. And, once this "roughly correct" form is mastered, the rest is up to the fighter and coach's talent. **While talented**

fighters can elevate this "roughly correct" form to one that's right for them and effective, it is over without talent.

So, what's the difference between a form that's "roughly correct" and one that's "effective"? It is whether that form allows you to exert power optimally. The form is a means, not an end, and the goal is to exert power optimally (and win the competition). This doesn't mean that form is unimportant.

Forms are an important frame of reference. They are movements that our predecessors have deemed, through competition (or fights in the martial arts), to be optimal for exerting power. Forms are the wisdom, ideas, and ingenuity of our predecessors crystallized. Thus, it would be difficult for some self-devised form from an ordinary person to defeat what's been built up over generations.

We just need to stand on the shoulders of giants. To stand on their shoulders and see further than them as a result. First, to learn the forms, then to tailor them to yourself. In this book, I want to provide you with a new tool—one that doesn't rely on talent—to make traditional forms work for you.

If we were to use the Power = Form x Fitness equation, this book focuses on the "x" (multiplication) part. It focuses on the part that ties together form and fitness.

A technical manual would explain the physical requirements in fine detail, such as "draw your arms in, externally rotate this area, and so on, to throw a strong punch," and introduce the optimal fitness regimen for that sport. This is based on the idea that you can generate a lot of power with the correct form and strength.

This book proposes the opposite.

First, we get to know power. Then, the body will derive the optimal form. This is because the goal is to exert power, not a beautiful form or physical fitness.

So, what do you need to do to throw a strong punch? You simply need to put your weight on the point where your punch lands.

And, while you do need optimal form and fitness to put weight behind your punch, you also need something that connects you to the ground: balance. **The "x" (multiplication) part that links form and fitness is balance, which is what connects you to the ground.**

Throwing a solid punch would be difficult on ice. The slightest shift in your center of gravity would make you fall. On ice, you wouldn't be able to perform the "roughly correct" form. You'd need to make minor adjustments to the form to maintain your balance.

Training that only breaks things down into form, strength, and so on ignores what ties it all together, or rather, what lies at the base of all this, which is the balance that keeps you grounded.

Human movement is complex. Just standing and moving on your two feet is impressive when you think about it. This is because a narrow 1- to 2-meter-long object can stand on two very small surfaces (the soles of your feet) and move around freely.

The foundation for human movement, not just in martial arts and sports, is balance—or your connection to the ground.

Just close your eyes and stand on one foot. You'll see that balance can't be explained by form or strength alone. What's needed isn't strength or the correct way to stand but an integration of these in the form of balance.

Too much focus on form and physical fitness is like discussing the delicate human system by hacking it into large chunks.

The Rubber Ball Power taught by the Zen monk is the ability to balance—to connect to the ground. Therefore, if we hone this ability, we should be able to strengthen our punches and kicks and launch the ball farther in ball games.

Birth of the Tripod Method

The Rubber Ball Power, the main theme of this book, is one of the secrets and fundamentals of martial arts. It is a form of balance that everyone possesses subconsciously and uses in all aspects of daily life. You experience it riding a bike or skiing down a slope, just in a different form. Even when you're just walking, you're using it without thought. Therefore, while the time required to acquire this power and everyone's skills may vary, anyone can learn to experience and use it. Yet, in the various martial arts that practice something like the Rubber Ball Power, I've seldom seen it explained as balance. The Tripod Method defines this power as a form of balance inherent in all of us and systematizes it through exercises that anyone can learn.

"Tripod" refers to the tripod used for cameras and so on. Tripods are stable because they contact the ground at three points. When we stand, we contact the ground at two points—the soles of our feet. And when you're pushed, you're contacting and receiving pressure from three external points: the place you're pushed and both soles of your feet. This system is called the Tripod Method because it allows you to remain stable and generate power in this situation.

In the next chapter and beyond, I will introduce the three principles governing this method, along with several exercises. The goal of this method is acquiring the Rubber Ball Power, and the three principles and exercises all aim to help you master this power.

While I call it the Tripod Method and the Rubber Ball Power, the three principles and exercises are all part of what the traditional martial arts teach. I have simply interpreted and expressed them in modern language. Nothing would make me happier than introducing you to a part of the profound martial arts world through this method.

When I compiled this method, I first had members of the Taikiken Buzenkai test it out. Most members grasped the basics in just one practice session. I also had women and the elderly with no martial arts experience test it out at a local cultural center where I teach, and the results were the same. And even though I'm limited to presenting to you on paper rather than in person, I believe you can gain the same understanding through this book.

The Rubber Ball Power, which you will master through the Tripod Method, is a form of balance inherent in everyone. Therefore, mastery is not directly correlated with time. It's the same as learning to ride a bicycle. Some people take a month, whereas others may get it within an hour.

When you get the hang of the Rubber Ball Power through the Tripod Method, you will suddenly get stronger. There are no changes to a person's body when they learn to ride a bicycle for the first time. However, there's an apparent difference between being able to ride a bike or being unable to do so. This is the same. The Tripod Method

<Figure 2-1> Surfing, for example, requires the ability to balance in situations where your footing is unstable.

doesn't require the time or change in physique it would take a person to increase their bench press from 50 kg to 100 kg.

Your ability to resist a push or, conversely, to push someone; your punching and kicking power; or driving the ball far in golf and baseball—underlying all of this is something that everyone possesses. It is balance, or the ability to connect to the ground. Muscle strength doesn't convert directly to force. It's just one of the elements necessary for the human body to stand and maintain balance.

A punch, for example, only transfers force to a subject when there is resistance from the ground. Throwing a punch while floating in space would reduce its power significantly. Standing in balance and

<Figure 2-2> In soccer and other sports, you must be able to balance while in contact with another player. The Tripod Method specializes in improving balance in such situations.

channeling the counterforce of the ground is the basis for movements such as hip rotation and hand speed.

So far, I've used the word "balance," which is often recognized as what's necessary to maintain your posture when your footing is unstable, such as when standing on one foot, riding a bicycle, or surfing. **<Figure 2-1>** But balance is also crucial when you're being pushed. A soccer player continuing to play while being tackled by other players is expressing this type of balance. **<Figure 2-2>**

When surfing or walking a tightrope, the shifting base destabilizes the body. On the other hand, when being pushed, the body is destabilized by the pressure from the point of contact. **The Tripod Method is a system**

specialized to improve your balance when facing external pressure.

The balance required for combat and other contact sports isn't the ability to balance on unstable surfaces, but one that allows you to maintain your posture when being pushed. In the martial arts, you may be taught something like the Rubber Ball Power, but it's rarely discussed in relation to balance. However, if we view this power as a form of balance, we can see that it's not something mysterious that can only be acquired through extensive training. Instead, it's something that's reproducible in a short amount of time.

Here's a summary:

▶ The Tripod Method's purpose/what you can gain from it:

The Rubber Ball Power = The ability to withstand a part of your body being pushed and to push back = Balance = The ability to connect with the ground

When you master this power with the Tripod Method, you will see improvements in the following abilities:

- **In ball sports, you will maintain your posture and continue playing while being tackled**
- **In combat sports, you will maintain your stance and not give in to your opponent's pressure**
- **You will use your opponents' force to break their postures**

- **Your punches and kicks will improve**
- **Your carry distance will increase in golf and baseball**

I will explain the specific methods from the next chapter, and now, I will introduce the three core principles of the Tripod Method.

The Three Principles of the Tripod Method

▶ 1. Leaning without leaning

This first principle is the power source of the Tripod Method (TPM). **The power you gain and use in the TPM isn't muscle strength. What is it, then? It's weight—your body weight.**

Your weight itself becomes the force you transfer. And to transfer your weight, you must lean on the point of contact between you and the subject before you. It'd be pretty heavy if a full-grown adult leaned on you. Dragging an inebriated friend back home is an ordeal. However, if you lean on someone fully, you'd lose your balance and fall if they removed their support. This is where "leaning without leaning" comes in. It's the feeling of leaning on the subject before you while leaning back to the same degree.

It's also the sense of leaning in all directions. When you lean in all directions, your center of gravity will fall straight down. **<Figure 2-3>** This can also be described as continuing to sink straight down while feeling the gravity, regardless of where you're pushed. When you lean

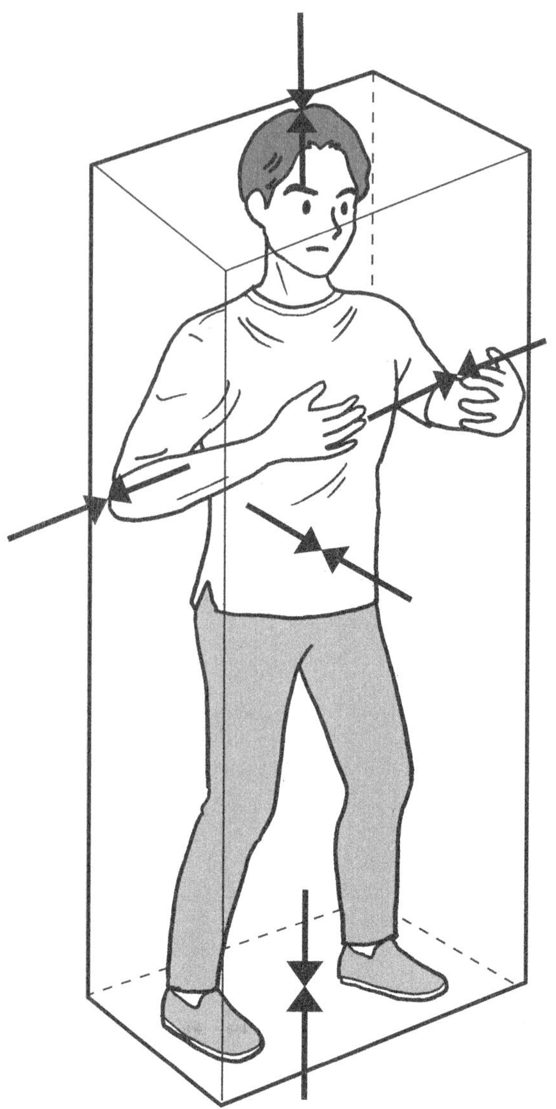

<Figure 2-3> Lean in all directions at the same time (up and down, front and back, left and right). Your center of gravity will then fall directly below you and provide stability.

in all directions, your body's axis will mostly be perpendicular to the ground, though this depends on which part of your body you use to lean on the subject. However, what's important isn't whether your body's axis is perpendicular or whether your posture is "good." What's important is whether you're leaning on the subject in front of you while leaning equally behind you. This will lead to stability as your center of gravity falls straight down. The reason why the first principle of the TPM is "leaning without leaning" and not "drop your center of gravity straight down" is because the latter makes it difficult to grasp the idea of putting your weight on various parts of your body (such as your arm, part of your torso, etc.).

There are expressions such as "a punch with weight behind it." How do you put weight behind a punch, and under what conditions can we say that weight has been put behind it? If you simply try putting your weight behind a punch, your body will tilt forward, and your posture will break. This would be fine if you just wanted to max out a punching machine at an arcade, but you can't repeatedly throw such a punch, and it is otherwise unusable.

However, if you can experience "leaning without leaning" and "leaning in all directions," you'll be able to put your weight on any part of your body, including your fist, while maintaining your balance. This isn't limited to your fists, shoulders, or other body parts, either. It's the same when putting your weight on the point of contact between your baseball bat or golf club and the ball. That is why the Tripod Method also increases how far you can hit the ball in various ball games.

Leaning without leaning = leaning in all directions = dropping your center of gravity straight down

This is the source of the power in the Tripod Method. The following two principles I'll cover are to transfer this power onto the point of contact between you and the subject while using as little muscle strength as possible.

2. Transferring force through bone

"Transferring force through bone" is about efficiently transferring the force generated with the first principle, "Leaning without leaning" (body weight), onto a subject. Let's try an experiment. Break a disposable chopstick in half down the middle without breaking it completely. The two halves are barely connected by wooden fibers. Try pushing its tip against something. If you push normally, the chopstick just bends at the break, and your force doesn't transfer to the point of contact. However, when you adjust the direction (angle) of your push, the angle of the break remains constant, and you can transfer your force to the tip of the chopstick. In other words, your force isn't cut off at the break. Put another way, the load isn't concentrated at the break. **<Figure 2-4>**

Many of the joints in the human body are either hinge joints, such as the elbows and knees, or ball-and-socket joints, such as the hip joints, with 360 degrees of movement. In other words, the human body consists of bones connected similarly to the broken chopsticks (It's more complicated, of course, but I won't get into the details here).

The biceps and triceps are the primary muscles for making a dumbbell curl movement with your arms. Therefore, you might believe that exerting a force with your arms bent would require strength from your biceps and triceps. However, like in the chopsticks experiment, if

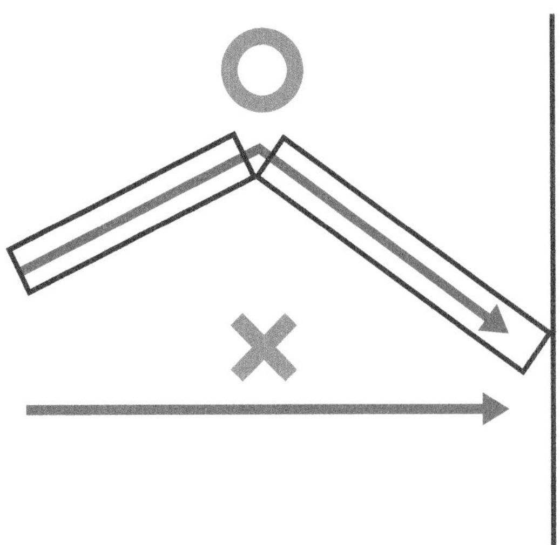

<Figure 2-4> You can push a broken and barely connected chopstick at a specific angle to allow your force to pass through to its tip.

you maintain the angle of your elbow, there's a specific direction (angle) in which you can transfer your force using almost no muscle strength. **<Figure 2-5>**

There's a secret to this. Your joints must be at an angle greater than 90 degrees. This is easy to understand with the chopstick. When you bend it past 90 degrees, you won't be able to push without straining the broken part (Though there's another way for angles less than 90 degrees). You can also feel this when doing a pushup. Pausing when your elbows are at an angle greater than 90 degrees isn't so hard, but it suddenly becomes much harder when your elbows flex more than 90 degrees. In Ritsuzen, the foundation of Taikiken, the arms are held in front of the chest as if

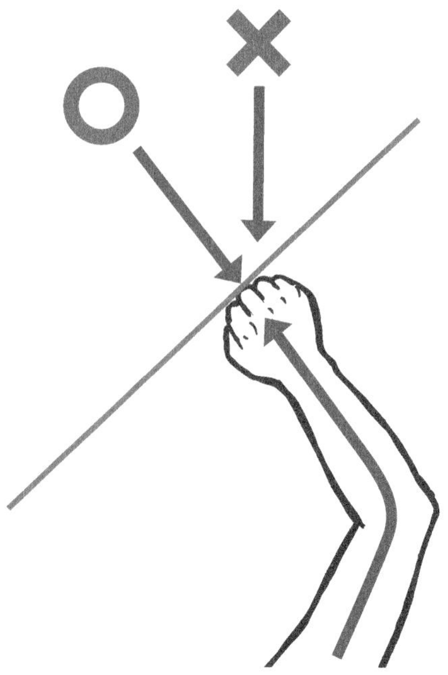

<Figure 2-5> Even with your elbow bent, you can transfer force in certain directions without using much arm strength.

hugging a ball, which also teaches you this optimal skeletal structure.

Your arm don't tire when you push a wall with straight arms. Usually, you can easily experience "transferring force through bone" when you fully extend your joints like this. However, fully extending your joints locks them in place when you want to move them, which makes them unadaptable and difficult to use.

As a side note, a basic rule is to not fully extend or flex your joints. You can only bend a fully extended arm and extend a fully flexed arm. Such a posture also has the disadvantage of making your next moves easy for your opponents to predict.

If you understand the relationship between angle and force through this chopstick experiment, you'll be able to transfer your power without using muscle strength, even when flexing your joints. Like in the above-mentioned pause during a pushup, this is something that all of us naturally feel and use in our daily lives. Therefore, all we need to do is to pursue our own form and consider how to generate power from this point of view.

3. The power of expansion and contraction

The first principle, "Leaning without leaning," enables you to use your body weight as a force. The second principle, "Transferring force through bone," allows you to transfer force onto a subject without using muscle strength. And the third principle is "The power of expansion and contraction." **Through this principle, you'll be able to exert more force, in all directions, simultaneously.**

Imagine a fire hose. The higher the water pressure inside the hose, the tauter it becomes and the more it tries to straighten out. This water pressure, the force straightening the hose, is the power of expansion.

Straighten your arm out in front of you. Imagine reaching out far with the tips of your fingers. Have someone push that arm from many directions. You'll find that your arm is hard to bend or move. This is sometimes explained as "the power of qi," as imagining qi flowing from your fingertips has the same effect. However, I believe referring to it as the power of qi is misleading. Anatomically, there aren't any channels in the body for qi, and it isn't qi that's making your arm strong and difficult to move. It's your muscles that are following your intention to straighten your arm and exerting themselves in a forward direction. As a result, your arm stiffens like a fire hose and becomes difficult to bend. It's easier to understand that it's muscle strength, not qi, passing through your arm. The difference between this and resisting a push as you might typically do, is the direction of your force. **Instead of fighting a push directly, you can best facilitate your extensors and other muscles by exerting a force in the forward direction, regardless of which direction you are pushed. <Figure 2-6>**

Regardless of the theory, this principle helps us understand power. To me, this experiment isn't about demonstrating the power of qi but about the effect of the direction you exert your force. Through this experiment, you can see that **straightening your arm generates resistance to forces from other directions.**

Here's an example. Raise your arms in front of your chest as if hugging a ball. This is the form for Ritsuzen. The fingertips of both your hands face each other. Now, imagine springs between the fingertips of both hands and try compressing them. If you have a training partner, have them hold the fingertips of both your hands, then apply force in the direction that opens the distance between your fingers.

As you resist by exerting force in the direction that closes the distance between your fingers, you'll see there's resistance when the outside of the ball (back of your hand) is pushed and, simultaneously, resistance when pushed from within the ball (palm of your hand).

You can also generate this feeling by imagining yourself hugging a ball. As you resist the ball expanding in your arms, power is generated

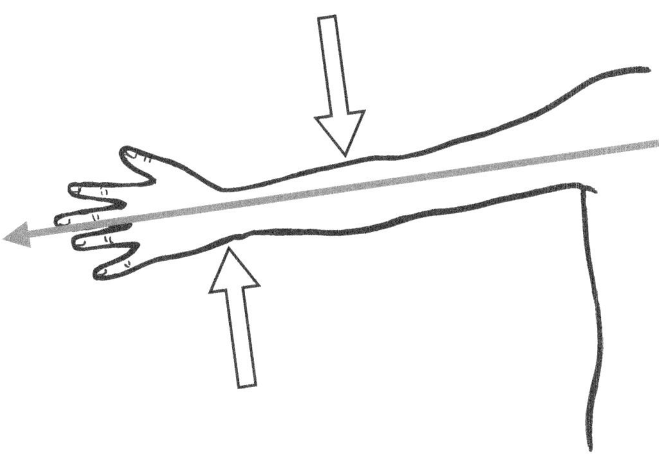

<Figure 2-6> When you extend your arm as if you were reaching far with your fingertips, your arm will be difficult to bend in any direction.

both inside and outside. If you credit this to the power of imagination, you'll mistakenly believe that you've gotten stronger due to some delusion. So I'll repeat: the imagery made your power flow towards your fingertips, generating power in both the inside and outside directions. It's the same principle as when a fire hose can withstand a push from any direction as its water pressure increases. The only difference is whether the power comes from water or your muscles.

Instead of directly opposing the force trying to bend your arm, exert your power straight toward your fingertips. You could also say that you're consciously using your extensor muscles (extending) instead of your flexor muscles (bending).

I explained using the arm because it's easy to understand, but this power is even more important in the vertical direction, from the top of your head to the soles of your feet. When you exert your power upwards, as if you were resisting a push from the top of your head, you'll be better able to withstand a push to your chest from the front or a push to your back from behind. This is because you're expanding (extending) in the vertical axis (while the power of contraction is also at work simultaneously). **<Figure 2-7>**

Additionally, if the back of your hand is pushed before you get a feel for this and your palm is suddenly pushed (pulled), you'll be pulled forward forcefully. This is because when you resist a force from one direction, there's a significant loss of power in the opposite direction.

Fighting force with force head-on will be used against you by your opponents. When setting up a hip throw, the thrower pushes the receiver, and when the receiver resists by shifting his center of gravity forward, they are thrown. Here, the thrower uses the receiver's power when the receiver pushes forward in response to being pushed back. This happens because the receiver can no longer resist being pulled forward by the thrower.

By using the power of expansion (power of extension) and the power of contraction, you'll be able to push and pull without losing your balance.

I've explained that mastering the Tripod Method will allow you to not lose when being pushed, and this means that you'll be able to maintain your balance when facing an external load.

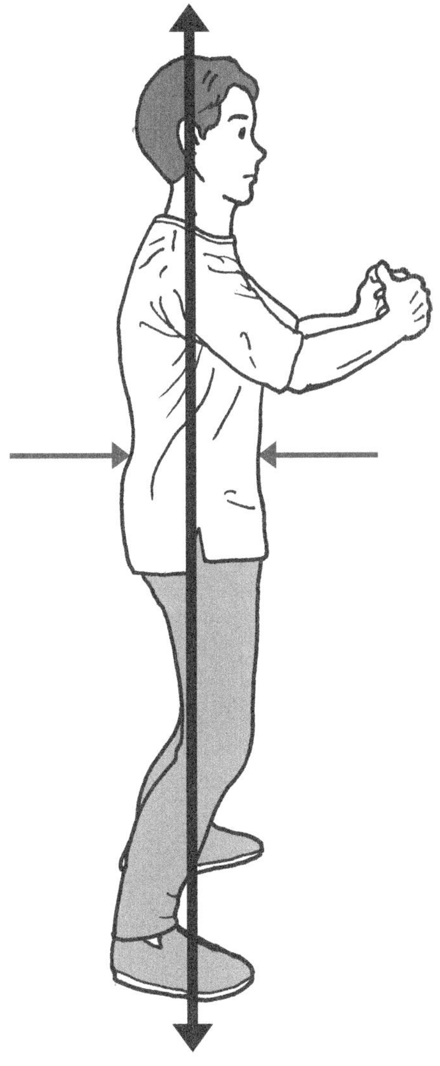

<Figure 2-7> Just like the example of using your arm as a hose, when you imagine your body extending up and down, you will be more resistant to being pushed or pulled.

Chapter 3

Mastering the Tripod Method

Experiencing the Tripod Method

In this chapter, I will introduce specific exercises to master the Tripod Method's three principles. **As the three principles are a distillation of some of what you can gain from these exercises, what's most important are these exercises.**

While putting things into words is essential for communication, it makes reality abstract and isolates only part of it. Principles are the epitome of this. They pretend to be the most important but may be the furthest things from reality. I hope you can have real experiences through these exercises, instead of something abstract, simplified, or one-size-fits-all.

Additionally, except for a few partner exercises, being competitive and trying to win is an inefficient way to practice. Every exercise has an objective, so focus on it and do each exercise to nurture one another.

The Tripod Method was developed with Taikiken at its core while drawing from various martial arts. Therefore, the three principles are simply an extract of what's been passed down in the martial arts since time immemorial. Also, the exercises I'm about to introduce are martial arts-based, so I recommend exploring the martial arts if you want to delve deeper (preferably Taikiken, if I may add my wish).

Exercise 1: Center Push

First, I would like you to try the following.

① Stand up straight, as if you were suspended from the crown of your head, not falling backward or forward. Then, join your hands below the navel and face each other.

② Now, slowly push each other with linked arms. <Figure 3-1>

Standing up straight and firmly is fundamental to both sports and everyday life. To check if you're standing firmly, see if you can take a push in the above posture without wobbling.

Many struggle to withstand their partner's pressure in this exercise and are pushed backward. Also, it will be challenging to push each other if you're both standing in an unstable posture. In this case, one person can push the other while staggering their legs.

Mastering the Rubber Ball Power will drastically improve the sense of stability in your body when pushing and being pushed.

▶ Developing the Rubber Ball Power

① Face each other, join your arms, and lean on your partner. <Figure 3-2>
Your training partner should support you such that if they removed their support, you would fall forward.

② Feel your weight at the point of contact between you

<Figure 3-1> Bring your hands together and push each other. You can check if you're standing firmly by how stable you are in this position.

<Figure 3-2> First, bring your hands together, make contact with your partner, and lean on them. Start in a posture where you would fall forward if your partner were to pull their hand away.

and your partner. Now, slowly inch your feet forward without removing your weight, or have your partner move forward slowly. Keep leaning.

③ **While keeping your weight on the point of contact between you and your partner, walk forward until you wouldn't fall forward if your partner removed their support.**

④ **Check your stability again, seeing if it has become easier to withstand a push.**

That is how you apply the Tripod Method's first principle, "Leaning without leaning." Once again, the power you're cultivating with the Tripod Method is nothing more than weight (body weight). So, first, simply lean on your partner and see if this creates a force that pushes your partner (Step 1). When you lean on your partner, they should feel quite a bit of weight (force). If you want to apply more pressure, deepen your lean and raise your arms. **<Figure 3-3>** In this case, because force will increase at the expense of balance, only do this to confirm that force = body weight. Make sure you're leaning with your body straight when doing this exercise. Bending forward at the waist only transfers the weight of your upper body to your partner, whereas bending backward only transfers the weight above your knees. **<Figure 3-4>** Leaning straight, as if the crown of your head and the soles of your feet were in a straight line, will maximize the weight transferred to your partner. This exercise also shows why correct posture is so emphasized in the martial arts.

You have now placed your weight on the point of contact between

<Figure 3-3> Deepen your lean to transfer more weight.

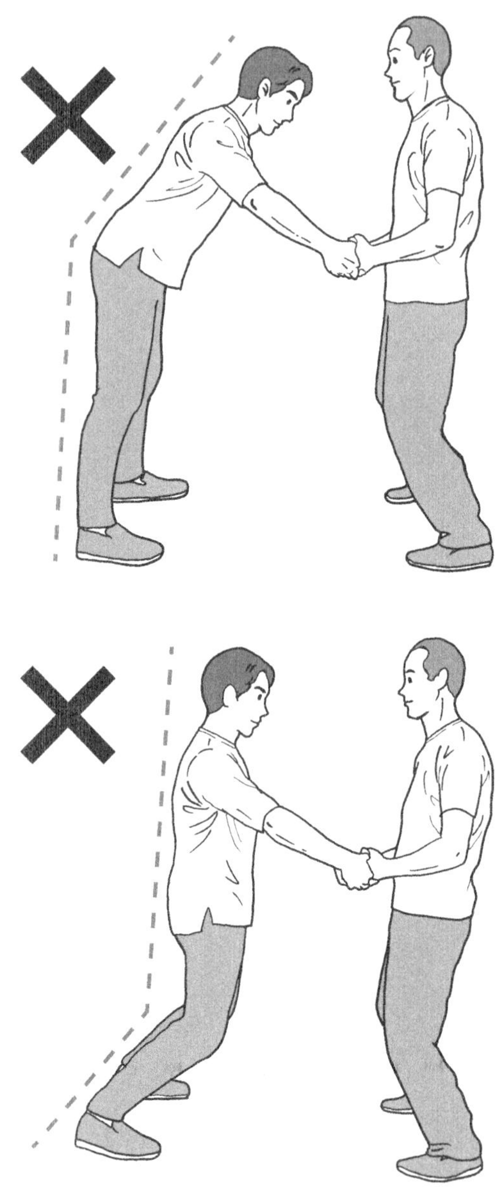

<Figure 3-4> When leaning, it's more difficult to transfer your weight to your partner if you bend forward or backward at the hips.

<Figure 3-5> Slowly walk forward while leaning. This will decrease the weight you transfer, but try to keep the sensation of leaning on the point of contact between you and your partner. This is how you stay stable when you're being pushed!

you and your partner. However, you would still fall forward if your partner pulled back. While many struggle with getting a feel for this next part, inch your feet toward your partner until your body is as vertical as possible, all while maintaining the sensation of leaning on your partner. **<Figure 3-5>** While your weight on the point of contact will decrease as you raise your body, you're doing this exercise correctly if you can preserve the sensation of having your weight on this point. I want you to keep leaning on your training partner's arms. Then, if you can walk forward until you're standing vertically, even if your training partner pulls back, you won't fall forward. At this point, if you can maintain the sensation of having your weight where you and your partner are in contact, your power—when pushed like before—will be on another level. When you get the hang of it, you can feel this leaning sensation anytime, even when you're not being pushed. You'll also be able to create this sensation anywhere in your body, not just in your arms. Also, you can try this exercise alone by pushing a wall, but you must feel that you would maintain your balance even if the wall were to disappear.

Exercise 2: Fist Push

① Get into a staggered stance with your training partner, face each other, then extend and bring your front fists together.

② Push each other in this position while maintaining your postures, without leaning forward. <Figure 3-6>

<Figure 3-6> Extend and join your fists and push each other while keeping your upper body straight.

Again, if you do this exercise with someone who has mastered the Rubber Ball Power, your entire body will be pushed back with your front foot lifting off the ground, or your arm will bend. If your arm bends, you might believe you lost due to a lack of arm strength—but that isn't true. You bent your arm because you sensed that if you didn't do so to absorb your partner's force, you would be lifted up and pushed backward. Therefore, it was your body that lost the push. Unlike the Front Push, because your legs are staggered, you can withstand more force, and even if you lean slightly forward, you're less likely to fall because your front leg is there to support you. As a result, compared to the Front Push, you're more likely to rely on your strength, lean forward, and push your training partner without maintaining your balance. Therefore, when trying this exercise, please keep in mind the main objective: developing a sense of "leaning without leaning." When you do this correctly, your upper body will naturally become almost perpendicular to the ground.

At first, it's good to lock your elbows out to focus on using your body weight without caring about your arm strength. Once you've grasped the feeling of putting weight on your fists, I'd like you to keep your elbow slightly bent. By bending your arm, it'll become easier to adapt when your partner changes the direction of their push. You'll also cultivate the Tripod Method's second principle, "transferring force through bone," where bending your arm doesn't necessarily mean you'll need muscle strength.

Because this exercise resembles the form for punching and fighting, it will also develop a stronger punch. If you can put weight on your fists in this exercise, you'll notice that you can also transfer more force to your opponent when striking. The more you lean your body, the more weight you can put on your opponent. However, your balance will suffer significantly with a deep lean, and you won't be able to move back or strike repeatedly. **The goal isn't to lean but to "lean without leaning" and to "lean in all directions."**

Supplementary Training

You can try this next exercise alone, against a wall. Lean on a wall with your fist while maintaining a feeling that you could continue standing without losing your balance if the wall were to disappear. **<Figure 3-7>** You'll be stronger and have a better balance if you stagger your legs. On the other hand, if you open your legs side to side, parallel to the wall, you won't be able to push the wall hard, but you'll feel your balance more delicately.

You could try an even better exercise if you have a balance ball (also known as a stability ball, exercise ball, Swiss ball, etc.). Try pushing a balance ball into the wall like you pushed your fist into the wall. As you increase your pressure, the ball will go off-center and become difficult to control. By continuing to push the ball while maintaining control, you'll develop both the feel for pushing and the ability to continuously hold down the center. This exercise is more challenging and fun using a smaller balance ball with a diameter of around 30 cm, as holding down the center will be more difficult. And, on top of the sense for holding down the center, you'll also learn how the ball escapes, giving you a sense of how to escape when you're pushed. Talk about learning the

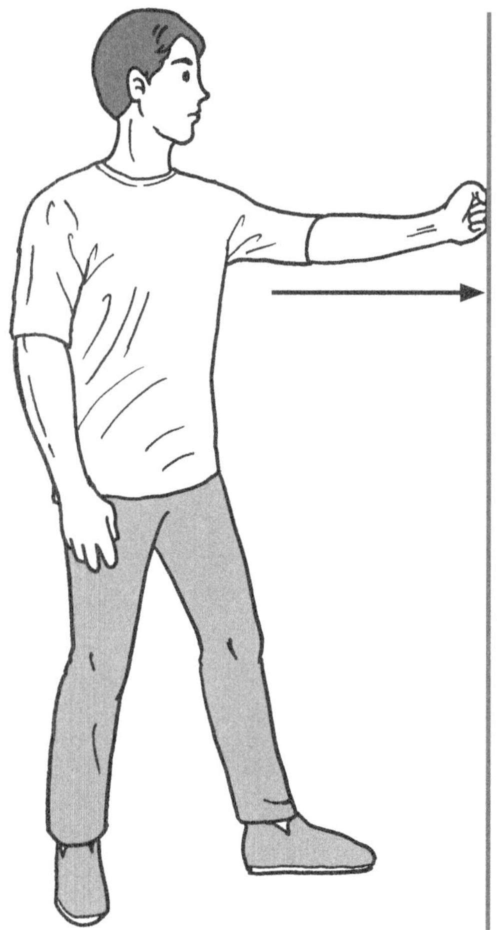

<Figure 3-7> You can practice without a partner by pressing your fist against a wall. Push the wall while maintaining your balance, so that you wouldn't fall if the wall were to disappear.

<Figure 3-8> If you do this with a balance ball between the wall and your fist, you can also develop the sense of holding down the center of your target. Additionally, if you strike the ball while holding it against the wall with your other hand, you will learn to strike in a way that allows the impact to penetrate your target without rebounding.

Rubber Ball Power from a rubber ball! **<Figure 3-8>**

For another exercise, try holding a small balance ball against a wall with one hand and punching it hard with the other. Your arm will spring back if you hit the ball normally. But try absorbing this impact and returning the vibration back to the ball. This isn't like a regular punch, where you pull back quickly to prepare for the next offensive or defensive move. You want to hold the ball down after hitting it. This exercise teaches you how to strike so that your opponent's body absorbs your impact. An impact is a vibration, or a wave. To transmit this wave (force) efficiently, avoid unnecessary tension in your body, allowing it to flow unhindered. However, focusing on this sensation too much can make your punch more like a push.

Exercise 3: Chest Push (Front, Staggered)

▶ Chest Push (Front)

① Stand face-to-face with your partner and place the backs of your hands on each other's chests.

② Push your partner while standing straight, not leaning forward. <Figure 3-9>

This is an excellent exercise to test the power of the ball in your arms that you can develop through Ritsuzen, which I will explain later. When I say the strength of the ball in your arms, you might think about

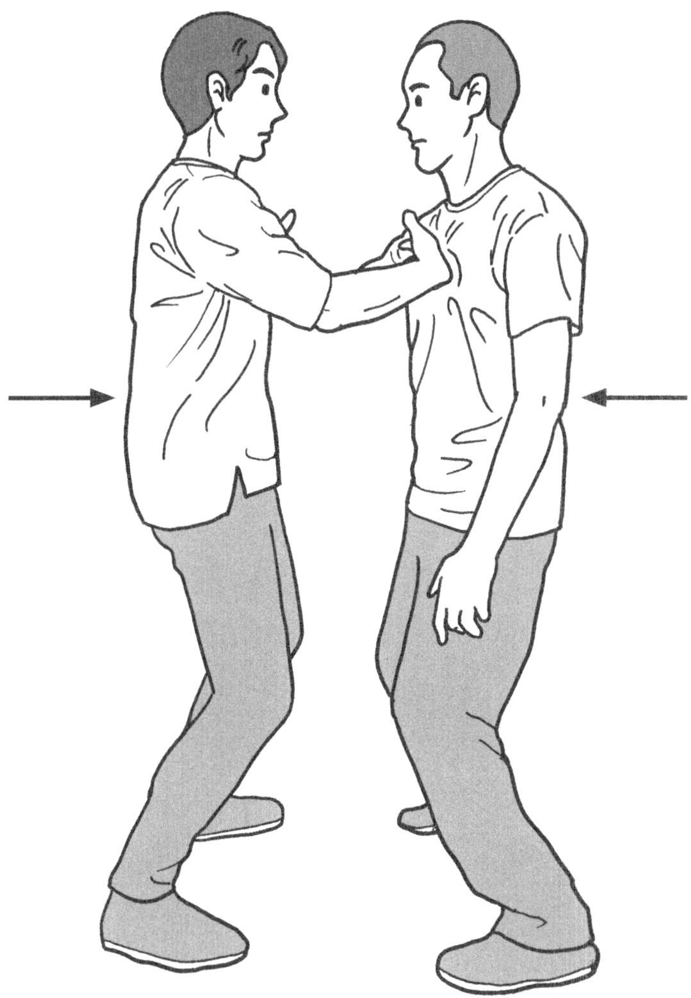

<Figure 3-9> Face each other and put the backs of one of your hands on each other's chests, and push while keeping your upper bodies straight. Focus more on your chest, which is being pushed by your partner, than on the back of your hand.

how tense your arms are or about arm strength, but when you do this exercise, you'll realize that your core strength is what's important. When you're pushing your partner's chest with the back of your hand, instead of focusing on your arm that's pushing your partner, focus on your chest that your partner is pushing with the back of their hand. If you can apply the power you experienced in the Front Push and Fist Push exercises to the point of contact between your chest and your partner's hand, you can unbalance your partner by simply extending your arm. This exercise shows that your core is what's essential, not your arms.

This is off topic, but Karl Gotch, known as the "God of Professional Wrestling," introduced the same exercise in an old magazine article.

▶ Chest Push (Staggered)

① Face each other with a staggered stance, front hands on each other's chests, and back hands holding each other's elbows.

② Push each other in this position, avoiding leaning forward as much as possible. <Figure 3-10>

Here, your points of contact are your palms, chests, and elbows. In this case, it's also better to generate the Rubber Ball Power in your chest (being pushed) rather than your palm (doing the pushing). If only one person has mastered the Rubber Ball Power, you'll notice that the other person won't be able to push or compete in strength, and they will be lifted up.

The Tripod Method is for exerting a force while remaining balanced

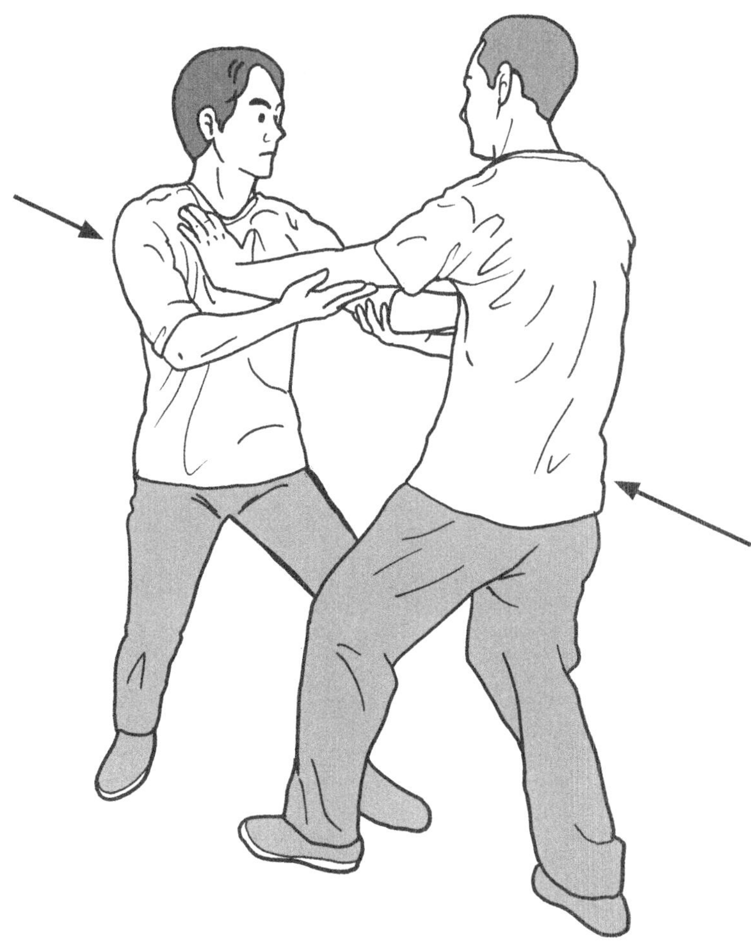

<Figure 3-10> Face each other in a staggered stance with your front hands on each other's chests and your back hands holding each other's elbows. Now, push each other while keeping your upper bodies straight. Focus more on your chest, which is being pushed, than on your front hand.

when being pushed. Therefore, once you master it, you'll get a feel for when your opponent is unbalanced and how to break their balance.

Exercise 4: Fist Walk

① Stand face-to-face with your partner and bring both fists together, positioning them at the sides of your waists. <Figure 3-11>
If pushing fist-to-fist is too painful, one side can receive with their palms.

② One side tries walking forward while avoiding leaning forward as much as possible. The receiver walks back while resisting. <Figure 3-12>

In this exercise, if you try to walk forward normally, you won't be able to do so if the receiver resists. When you lift a leg to step forward, you will lose to your partner's force. This is because you lost the Rubber Ball Power when moving. I want you to walk forward while focusing on maintaining the sense you developed in a static exercise like the Front Push, even as you move. You'll often lose your power when you're not used to doing this, particularly in your arms, such as your shoulders and elbows. The difference between before and after you can do this exercise is obvious. You won't be able to move forward before you get it, no matter how hard you push, but once you get it, you'll be able to move forward with ease, as if your partner weren't even there. This exercise is

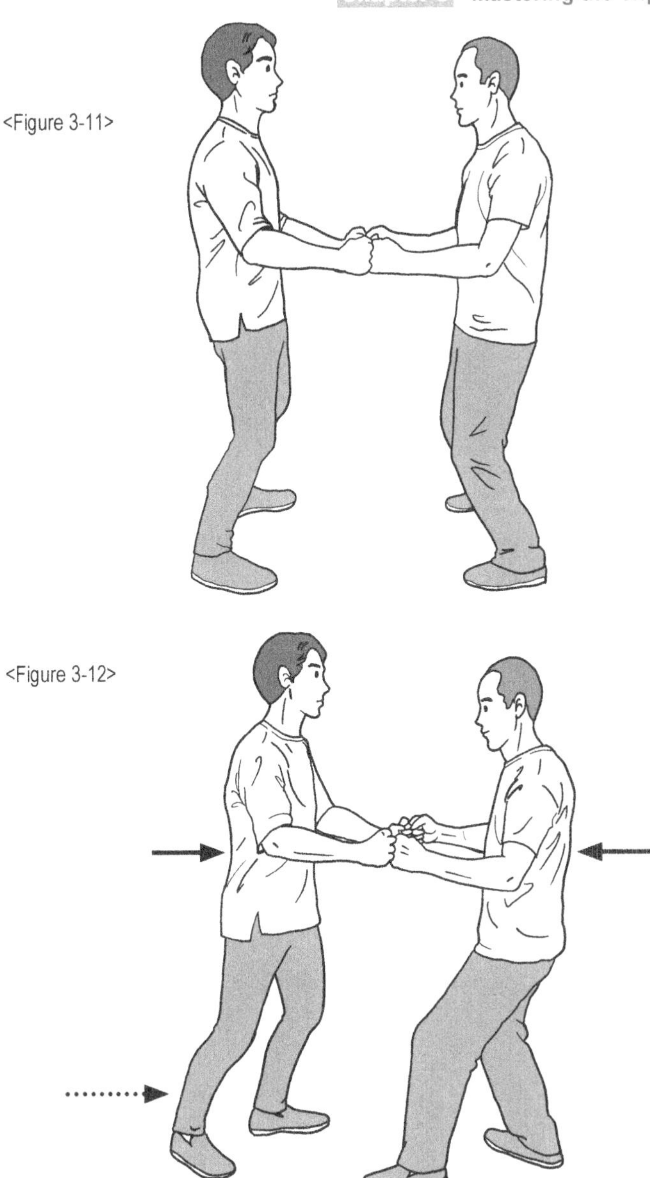

<Figure 3-11>

<Figure 3-12>

Bring your fists together at waist level, and one of you will walk forward while both of you keep your upper bodies straight. The person who isn't walking forward will walk backward while resisting. Walking forward will be very easy when you master the Rubber Ball Power.

also an excellent way to get a feel for moving with your entire body. I recommend a narrower stride because a wider stride makes this exercise more challenging.

Exercise 5: Front Arm Push

① Face each other in a staggered stance and bring your front forearms together.
② Push each other while trying to maintain balance. <Figure 3-13>

The Front Arm Push is the starting position for Tuishou, a widely practiced exercise in Chinese martial arts. In Tuishou, the arms are rotated back and forth elliptically, with you and your partner's forearms in contact. While you shouldn't use too much strength in Tuishou, you simply want to push each other in this exercise.

If you use your arm strength to push your partner's forearm, your shoulder area will quickly become tired. Here, you can lean firmly on your partner's forearm. However, if you lean forward as usual, you'll lose your balance if your partner withdraws their forearm. Therefore, while leaning on your forearm, you must simultaneously lean back on your head and back. It should feel as if you're pushing your partner's forearm while exerting pressure on the back of your body. This keeps your upper body perpendicular to the ground, even as you lean on your partner's forearm. In other words, this is the first principle: "Leaning

<Figure 3-13> Face each other in a staggered stance, bring your front arms together, and push each other while keeping your upper bodies straight. While leaning forward (on your partner's front arm), simultaneously hold the sensation of leaning backward.

without leaning" and "Leaning in all directions." To see if you're doing this correctly, have your partner suddenly remove their arms while you're pushing each other. You want to keep your ground at that moment without fully extending your arm or falling forward. While your arm might momentarily extend toward your partner, it should immediately return to its original position. At that point, you'll feel an elasticity in your arm, like a rubber ball or spring. When you master the Rubber Ball Power, your whole body will react like a rubber ball—with elasticity.

In this exercise, simply being strong in the forward and backward directions doesn't mean you'll overpower your partner. **What's important is maintaining your center by applying the Rubber Ball Power in every direction—up, down, front, back, left, right—and having a sense of your center as a result.**

Exercise 6: Tenchi Saiki (Heaven and Earth Qi Cultivation)

You can do this exercise alone to strengthen the Rubber Ball Power.

① Starting in front of your chest, raise both arms through the center of your body. <Figure 3-14-1, 2>

② Expand your arms as if you were taking in a deep breath, then start squatting down. <Figure 3-14-3, 4, 5>

③ When you reach the bottom, raise your arms through your center and start standing. <Figure 3-14-6, 7>

There's a similar movement in Qigong, but the difference here is that you should try not to wobble no matter where someone were to push you. If you apply the Rubber Ball Power where you're pushed, you should create a resistance like in the previous exercises. Also, while you'd never sink this low in a typical martial arts stance, this is an excellent exercise to see if you can maintain your power even when your body is in its lowest position. It's an effective way to check if your crouching position is correct (has power). Also check if you have power (if you don't wobble when pushed) when your body and arms are fully extended at the top. When performing this exercise, imagine your body filling with qi as your knees and arms extend and then expelling qi from throughout your body as you squat down. This movement is difficult as your body goes from fully extended to fully contracted, but it's a highly effective exercise that stimulates your full vertical range of motion. You can experience the essence of the Rubber Ball Power with this exercise, such as how your body weight powers it and the importance of your weight dropping straight down.

I initially called this exercise the Deep Breath Squat because I was worried that giving it a mystical name would hide the source of its power. But that was too bland and misaligned with its purpose, so I went with Tenchi Saiki. In reality, the sensation of filling your body with qi will give you a sense of your center of gravity, relax your limbs, and give you a grasp of the natural flow of power.

1
2
3
4
5

<Figure 3-14> Imagine your body filling with energy as you raise your arms, then expelling this energy as you squat down. Maintain the Rubber Ball Power throughout this movement.

Exercise 7: Ritsuzen

① Stand straight as if you were suspended from the crown of your head, loosen your knees lightly, and keep your feet around shoulder width apart.

② Raise your arms in front of your chest as if you were hugging a ball. <Figure 3-15>

I hope you could feel the Rubber Ball Power through the first five exercises. After that, I want you to continue with an exercise that will elevate this power. In Tenchi Saiki, you develop the ability to harness this power while in motion. By fully expanding and contracting your

<Figure 3-15> Ritsuzen is the most important way to develop the Rubber Ball Power. Imagine hugging a ball in front of your chest.

body, from deep knee flexion to full extension, the exercise cultivates the Rubber Ball Power (your ability to control your center of gravity) in every position.

And in this book, I would like to introduce Ritsuzen as the most important exercise. In fact, an entire book could be written on Ritsuzen alone and what you can gain from it. And while it's an incredibly beneficial Qigong exercise for both mental and physical health, I'd like to introduce it in this book with a focus on developing the Rubber Ball Power, or your ability to exert power in all directions (and resist it from all directions). If you want to learn more about Ritsuzen, I recommend the DVD by my master, Michio Shimada, or the books by Masters Satoshi Amano and Seiji Sato.

Here are a few key points:

① **Stand as if you were suspended from the crown of your head by a rope (around the pressure point known as Bai Hui). And loosen your body so that you're not pulled up. Sink down, as if you were sitting down. Even though you're sinking, your posture doesn't change much because the rope pulls you up. Conversely, the crown of your head is touching the ceiling and being pushed down. You extend your body up to not be crushed. These two forces and images seem contradictory, but they are not (I will go over the subjective and objective sides of power in more detail later).**

② **Keep your eyes open. Looking far, taking everything in.**

Your facial expression, between smiling and not smiling. Your mouth, between open and closed, starting to salivate. Breathing naturally, without trying to deepen or speed up your breath. Your temples, the space between your brows, and the back of your head unwind on their own, creating a sense of ease. Your facial expression is very important. A relaxed face helps your body relax. When doing Ritsuzen as a martial arts practice, it's easy to adopt a stern facial expression, so watch out for this.

③ Your throat, as if you were drinking pure and delicious water. Your chest is relaxed as if you just sighed. Not raising your shoulders, forcing them down, rounding them, or sticking your chest out.

④ Your arms should be in front of your chest with your palms around shoulder height but don't worry about this too much. You are hugging a ball in your arms, trying not to drop it. Holding it gently to avoid crushing and breaking it. Holding large softballs in both hands, glass marbles between your fingers, and baseballs between both armpits—without dropping or breaking them. There's a spring between each opposing finger. You're trying to squeeze them together—you're trying to stretch them apart.

⑤ Neither rounding nor arching your back. Relaxing your belly, creating a sense of fulfillment. As if a vertical pole was coming out of your perineum (the area between the genitals and anus), and you were sitting on it. Your hip joints naturally loosen.

⑥ Lightly loosen your knees. You feel an external rotation at your feet when you sink down (left foot turning anti-clockwise and right foot turning clockwise) and an internal rotation when you stand up, but don't open or close your knees. A bolt has threads cut into it, but it is straight. That's the image. Your center of gravity at the soles of your feet should be around the Yong Quan (just in front of the arches), but this can change depending on your posture.

⑦ I emphasize relaxing because your muscles can't help but tense when you're standing with your arms raised in Ritsuzen. If you only want to relax, you can just lie down and unwind. But you're not trying to let go fully because the human body can't move without muscle tension. You're aiming for as little tension as possible.

⑧ Your whole body feels as if you were underwater. This means your whole body feels a slight resistance in every direction. This is the same as trying not to drop or break the ball or pushing and pulling the springs. You don't need to use much force at all. Just thinking about it is good enough.

It is an ambiguous expression because there's an awareness of the opposing directions in every movement. For example, your elbows are trying to extend and flex simultaneously. This means that your biceps and triceps are both receiving nerve impulses to move (contract). The muscles throughout your body are all quietly active in this way. Every muscle and nerve in your body is both resting and active.

⑨ In general, keep the joints at obtuse angles (greater than 90°). The reason for this is structural and can be understood in a pushup, where a lot of muscle strength is required when your elbows are bent deeply, as explained in the "Transferring force through bone" section.

⑩ Imagine someone nudging you from various directions and see if you can summon the Rubber Ball Power. If you have a training partner, they can lightly touch the backs of your hands, the back of your head, and other parts of your body to see if there is power. While a training partner makes it easier to feel, imagining the resistance also has advantages. For example, you can instantly create an opposing force in any direction and adjust its strength. For instance, you could use your imagination to make the ball lighter or heavier or the water pressure higher or lower. You'll then notice small

changes in your muscle tension, posture, and so on in response to your imagination.

While there are many other cues, if you start with too many, you'll become confused and end up doing the opposite of what Ritsuzen seeks to achieve. Start with:

- **Taking it easy**
- **Being suspended from the crown of your head and loosening your knees**
- **Softly hugging the ball in your arms**

Being aware of just these points is good enough.

The Office Chair Experiment

I'll now introduce some effective ways to help you understand the power of the TPM.

Pushing a table while sitting in an office chair

If you have a freely moving chair, such as an office chair with casters on its legs, you can feel what it means to "connect to the ground." Sit in that chair and try pushing a table or wall in front of you with both legs off the ground. As your arms extend, your body will likely roll back with the chair. **<Figure 3-16>**

<Figure 3-16> Sit on a chair with wheels and push against a desk (or wall). How would you push the desk hard in this situation?

This is because the wall's counterforce is working in the direction opposite to the wall, or behind you (the law of action and reaction). Try to push the wall harder in this situation without being pushed backward. If you use the wall to push your body down, as if you were holding the casters down from above, the counterforce will point downward, away from the direction the casters roll. You can now push the wall harder without rolling back. This is what earthing, or transferring power to the ground, feels like. If your body, which is between the wall and the chair, absorbs the force flexibly, you will feel like a rubber ball, and if you

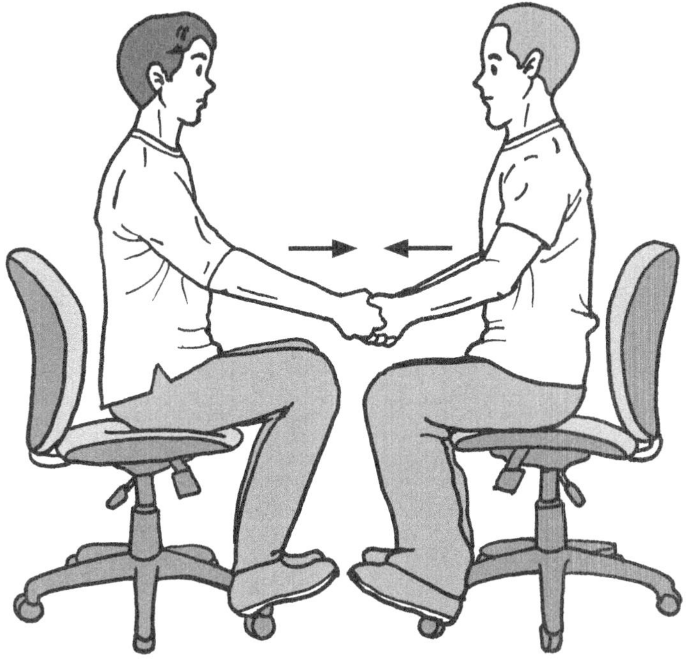

<Figure 3-17> Push each other in this situation and find the best way to push with force.

tense up, you will feel like a stake coming out of the ground.

Also, pushing the wall directly in front of you will simply push you back, but if you take one hand and push a little to the left or right of you (to the right with your right hand, to the left with your left hand), the office chair will spin. In this case, to generate a force directly downward to push hard against the wall, you must also exert a force in the direction that prevents your hip (chair) from spinning. When testing this, you'll feel a strong pressure in your left butt when pushing with your right hand. From this, you can feel that power from the right hand comes from the left hip and leg, while power from the left hand comes from the right hip and leg. If you have two office chairs, you can also do a fun partner exercise by facing and pushing each other while sitting in the office chairs with your legs off the ground. **<Figure 3-17>**

Upper Wall Push

① Raise both arms straight above your head.

② Lean forward in this position with both hands on the wall. <Figure3-18>

③ Gradually increase your lean angle while keeping your arms and body straight. <Figure 3-19>

▶ Variation

④ Gradually bring both arms, which are raised above your head, in front of your body. <Figure 3-20>

The source of the Tripod Method's power is the power of gravity falling perpendicularly.

You then use the sense of "leaning without leaning" and "leaning in all directions" to apply this power in all directions. All directions here refer to up, down, forward, backward, left, right, and every other direction. And the most important of these are the up and down directions. While leaning upward and leaning downward are awkward expressions, I hope you get a feel for it through this exercise.

<Figure 3-18>

<Figure 3-19>

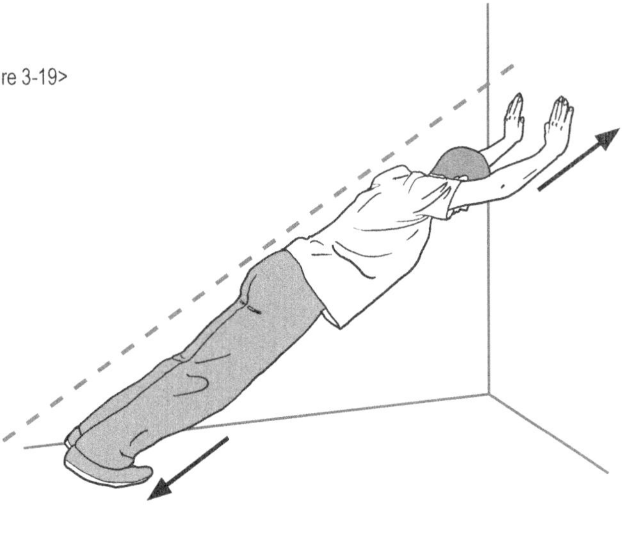

Lean against a wall with your body straight and gradually deepen your lean.
Imagine creating a tension rod with your entire body.

<Figure 3-20> Bring your arms, extended above you, to the front of your body. Even in this position, become a tension rod between the floor and wall, just like in the previous exercise. If you bend at your hip, your force will likely be interrupted there.

The wall, where your hands are, is right above your head from your perspective. In this position, you can put a lot of pressure on the wall with your hands. The force here, as usual, is mainly the weight of your body leaning against the wall. I want you to feel this through the expressions "leaning upward" and "leaning downward." You could also say applying your weight in the upward and downward directions.

Due to your body's structure, you can withstand much more force in the vertical direction than in the forward and backward directions. While you can already push the wall hard by simply leaning with a straight body and arms, you can push the wall even harder if you stand on your toes and stretch your entire body as if you were reaching up to touch the sky. Imagine a tension rod stretched diagonally between the wall and ground. Which parts of your body are tense when doing this? You'll notice that tension isn't concentrated in your arms, legs, or hips, but distributed evenly throughout your body. And that each body part is exerting itself proportionately to its strength. No muscle is overworking or slacking off. In this position, your arms, which are usually tense, realize their weakness, and depend on the hips and other body parts to exert power.

What's most important here is the positioning of your hips. **Your body won't be like a rod if your hips are bent, and your power won't be transferred.** It will weaken the feeling of leaning up and down, and your body will tense unnecessarily. When you play with bending and straightening your hips, you'll get a sense of when power is lost in your hips. This is the same idea as pushing a wall with a bent stick, where the load concentrates at the bend and the stick breaks. Also, if your hips are bent, only the weight above your hips is transferred to the wall. The

Tripod Method's second principle, "Transferring force through bone," showed that there's an angle at which you can still push hard with a bend. But here, it's easier to grasp the feeling of force being transferred from your arms to your legs if your body is straight. With practice, you can take many shapes while maintain this feeling of force being transferred.

This vertical force is fundamental for everything else. That's what variation ④ allows you to experience. Bring your arms, which are extended upward, toward the front of your body. When you do this, you will gradually understand that the force you feel up and down is the same when directed forward. You must simply become like a tension rod between the ground and the subject. Tension rods aren't held in place by a spring or other force. Instead, once their lengths are adjusted, the strength of their materials supports the walls. While your body is slanted in this exercise, gravity always exerts itself vertically. I want you to get a sense of your slanted body transferring this vertically oriented gravity (body weight) to the wall. When you understand this, you'll have a better feel for transferring your weight onto those you contact.

Chapter 4

Exploring the Rubber Ball Power

Move as If Your Whole Body Was One Muscle

I hope you could experience the Rubber Ball Power through the three principles of the Tripod Method and the exercises.

While it takes time to acquire an ability you've never had, this power is one that everyone possesses. In everyday language, the Rubber Ball Power is simply balance. The ability to deal with external pressure, such as when someone pushes you, is nothing more than balance. But balance generally suggests the ability to maintain your posture when your footing is unstable, such as when surfing or walking a tightrope.

On the other hand, because you tense up when pushed, you may believe that muscle strength and power, rather than balance, are what's required. But this is a misunderstanding. **<Figure 4-1>** Standing in place without compromising your posture when you're pushed, retreating, and not falling forward when your opponent creates space as you push back—these are all expressions of balance. Maintaining an awareness of your balance is crucial when engaging in a pushing match or trying to unbalance your opponent.

At first glance, the Rubber Ball Power may seem like some extraordinary power unrelated to balance, as it gives the body an elasticity to repel and redirect external forces.

The essence of the Rubber Ball Power, however, is harmony with gravity, or in other words, balance. And both the three principles and exercises are guidelines for positioning your body to maintain that balance.

I say the Tripod Method and Rubber Ball Power do not rely solely

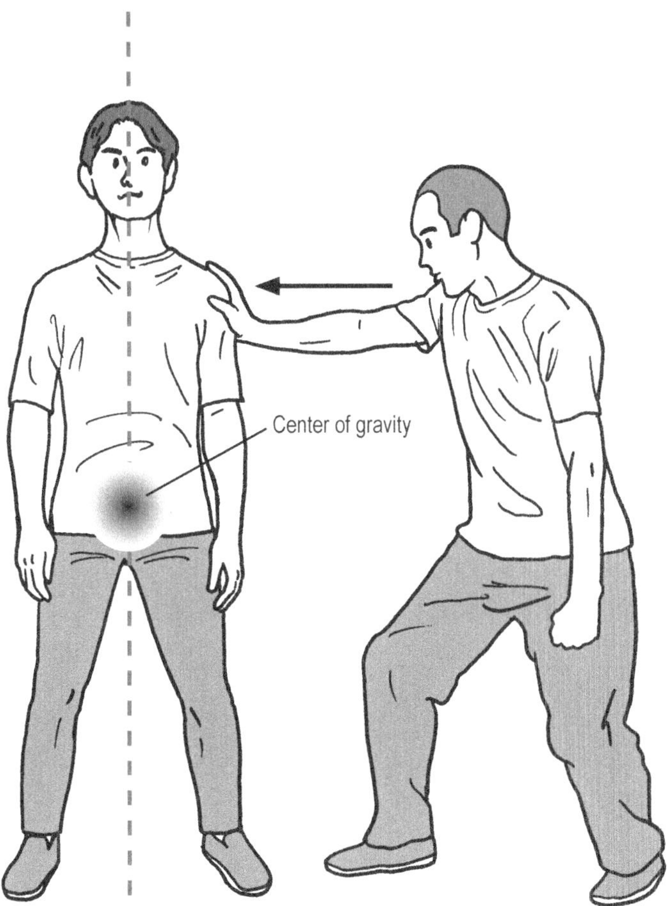

<Figure 4-1> The Rubber Ball Power is the balance that prevents your posture from collapsing, even when you are pushed. This doesn't come from muscle strength, but from keeping control of your center of gravity.

on strength because they are powered by balance. Take, for example, the ability to continue playing while being pushed by another player in soccer or rugby, without losing your posture. While this does require muscle strength, it demands more than that. Or, when standing on one leg with your eyes closed, no matter how well-developed the muscles of your legs, hips, or whole body, you wouldn't expect to stand for long periods with just that.

In other words, **muscle strength doesn't directly provide resistance to impact; instead, it's a secondary requirement to maintain a balanced posture (body structure) and center of gravity.**

If we consider your muscles as springs, hundreds of springs must work together as a single unit, one large spring, to maintain your posture. **You want to move as if your whole body were one muscle.**

The same applies to forms in the martial arts and the "correct" forms in each sport. They aren't ends in themselves. Their original purpose is to keep you balanced so you can perform stably in competition. That's why, now and then, a top-tier athlete with a unique and unconventional style emerges. They keep their balance with their own postures and movements. What's important aren't forms, which are considered universal, but a posture that's appropriate for a particular person and situation.

The Tripod Method is for developing the ability to remain still when pushed and the sense of maintaining your balance.

Generating Power from the Belly

In Japanese, there's an expression, to "generate power from the belly."

Since ancient times, Japanese people have regarded a thick belly as a good thing, with expressions like futoppara ("thick-bellied"), which means "generous," hara ga suwatte iru ("the belly is seated"), which means "composed," and hara ga juujitsu shite iru ("the belly is full"), which has a connotation of being "at ease." We also have a culture that regards the belly as the seat of the soul, with expressions like haraguroi ("black-bellied"), which means "malicious," and hara ni ichimotsu ga aru ("have a plot in the belly"), which means to have a hidden agenda. It may be a stereotype to say that the West is a culture of the heart, while the East is a culture of the belly. However, when practicing Eastern martial arts, many forms drop the center of gravity to the belly. When you raise your center of gravity to your chest (heart), you become mobile. And when you drop it, you become stable. The boxing stance makes you feel nimble, whereas the karate stance makes you feel solid. One reason is the difference in their centers of gravity.

I believe while modern Japanese people may be familiar with the expression "generating power from the belly," they don't feel it in their bodies. They primarily use their hands and arms to exert power at the point of contact with the opponent (subject).

So, when can you say you've generated power in your belly and transferred this power to your opponent through your arms?

You can also experience generating power from your belly through the Tripod Method.

Generating power from the belly is more than just rotating the hips and abdominal region and using that power. Your belly can generate power even if it appears still, and in fact, there's a certain type of power it can generate when it is still.

So, what does it mean to generate power from the belly?

Generating power from the belly is the ability to firmly establish your center of gravity and transfer your weight onto a subject.

For example, if your arms stretch forward while your hips remain back when wanting to push your opponent hard, your legs aren't supporting your arms. When you can feel your legs supporting your arms through your abdomen and use your arms as a passageway for power rather than its source, you'll distribute the load of pushing your opponent to not only your arms but also your belly and legs. The sensation here is nothing more than what I've repeatedly described in this book as "leaning without leaning," "transferring your weight to your opponent," or "supporting yourself with your opponent's body (without fully relying on it)."

If you look up the word heppirigoshi in the Daijirin, a Japanese dictionary, you get "An unstable half-squat posture with an anterior pelvic tilt." It also has similar connotations to the expression "weak-kneed." Freestyle wrestling stances, rugby scrums, and tackles are also performed in a half-squat position with the hips back and face forward, but heppirigoshi wouldn't be used to describe these athletes. Indeed, heppirigoshi is not about how a posture looks but about whether the hips can transfer the force received by the upper body to the legs. In the case of heppirigoshi, force is interrupted at the hips and doesn't transfer to the legs. In other words, you won't be able to bear that force.

Generating power from the belly also feels like you're generating power from your entire body. On the other hand, you might feel like you're not producing power anywhere in your body. This sensation arises when you use large muscle groups such as your legs or core to generate the same amount of power you would using your arms or another part of your body.

The Rubber Ball Power Is a Central Power

You'll initially feel the Rubber Ball Power experienced in the Tripod Method as an expansive power that pushes your opponent. When you expand, the front of your body moves forward, the back of your body moves backward, the top of your head moves up, and the soles of your feet move down. In other words, there is power in opposing directions, and if opposing directions exist, there must be a center somewhere that separates them.

If you're pushing forward with no power to the back, you will fall forward when your opponent pulls back. The Rubber Ball Power, which consists of power in all opposite directions, will allow you to generate power spherically (up, down, front, back, left, and right) with you at the center. You will then feel as if your body were stretching out, growing, and expanding. But the opposite is also true: if you experience power expanding in all directions, you will also notice power contracting towards your center. This power pulls your opponent in. When you push your opponent in front of you with your arms, your back pushes back behind you. This is what expansion feels like.

On the other hand, when you pull, your body moves forward as you pull your arms back. When you feel this expansion and contraction as you stand straight and still, your center is approximately at the lower dantian.

The center we discuss in the Tripod Method isn't conceptual or mental; it's a physical center—the center of balance. It's the same sensation you get when riding a bicycle. When riding stably, your center of gravity is close to the saddle; however, when turning or leaning your bike, your center of gravity shifts accordingly. So, while your center (center of gravity) does exist, it's constantly shifting and not fixed.

Moreover, it shifts when you contact an opponent or object (e.g., a sword, bat, or golf club). Your center isn't simply your own; it results from your balance as you encounter objects, centrifugal force, and so on. Therefore, if you look at a still image of something in motion, like in a photograph, it may appear unbalanced. However, this is a misunderstanding caused by not accounting for other forces. For example, it would be impossible to capture the true teachings of a martial arts master through breakdown images.

Humans can never escape the physical laws of nature. Therefore, you could say that any form is already in perfect accordance with nature's laws. But when your sense of center becomes clearer through the Tripod Method, your strength and balance will undoubtedly improve in various sports because **the Rubber Ball Power is a form of central power.**

Suspended from Above: The Power of Axes

The importance of the dantian and axis is often emphasized in martial arts. They make up the basis of movement. It wouldn't be an exaggeration to say that developing this sense is synonymous with creating form. **The Rubber Ball Power is a power from the center,** and the dantian can be felt as this central point. And when you expand your awareness of it, you will also get a sense of your axis.

The first of the three Tripod Method principles is "Leaning without leaning," or "Leaning in all directions." Leaning might give you the image of resting your weight against a wall in front or behind you. However, the sense of leaning above and below is more important. This means leaning on the ground and the ceiling pressing down on the crown of your head. While leaning on the ground is an unnatural expression, I want you to understand this as releasing your weight onto the ground. Just standing straight and releasing tension will release your weight onto the ground, which is good enough for now. Leaning on the crown of your head is another unnatural expression. Here, imagine the crown of your head touching the ceiling and exerting an upward pressure on it.

Step firmly on the ground and support the sky. This is the main sensation of the vertical axis. With just this, however, your axis will feel like a log as thick as your body rather than a fine line. When you combine this with leaning forward, backward, left, and right, your sense of power will gather at your center, and your axis will become a thin line. This is because when you lean forward and backward, you'll sense a surface separating the front and back of your body. And the same applies for the left and right directions. This line separating your power to the front, back, left, and right is a central line that can firmly resist a push from any direction. This is the sense of axis in the Tripod Method. In addition, adding the upward and downward division of power will make the vertical and horizontal lines cross to create a sensation near the dantian.

You can also feel your axis with the second principle, "Transferring force through bone." As you saw in the broken chopstick experiment, you can bend your joints and maintain that angle with little to no muscle strength for loads from certain angles and directions. For example, if your knees were only slightly bent, you could stand for a long time without feeling a strain in your thighs. And your spine also supports the weight of your head despite being arched.

Imagine standing relaxed with your knees loosened and carrying something heavy on your head. You create a natural axis when you can maintain this with good balance. Since ancient times, humans worldwide have carried objects on their heads in a method called head-carrying—it's precisely this feeling.

The location of your axis will also change with your posture. For instance, if you're crouching with your face forward like in a wrestling stance or rugby scrum, your axis will be toward the front of your body. Thus, it's not always along your spine or core. Your axis isn't fixed—it's a physical sensation based on the perception of your center of gravity. **And in the Tripod Method, I refer to this sense of axis as "vertical power," and consider it fundamental to generating power in the forward, backward, left, and right directions.** While the Rubber Ball

Power expands and contracts spherically, this vertical power, or power to stand, is essential to movement and power in the forward, backward, left, and right directions.

This vertical power can also be likened to the suspension of a car. A car's suspension uses the power of springs to maintain an appropriate pressure of the tires on the ground, thereby maintaining friction (propulsive power). **Our ability to move forward and backward is also closely related to the friction between the feet and the ground.** On ice, no man, no matter how strong or heavy, could push any woman on normal ground. Vertical power is precisely suspension. By applying pressure to the soles of your feet in the appropriate direction, you create friction with the ground, allowing you to push or strike your opponent. A car's suspension uses springs, hydraulics, or air pressure. Therefore, you cannot change the pressure easily. Humans, however, have a brilliant mechanism that could be called "mind-pressure suspension," which you can adjust at will through muscle tension and the angle of your bone structure.

The Rubber Ball Power is based on the perception of the dantian and axis, which make up your center.

Transfer Force Without Straining

When I first met the Zen monk who inspired the Tripod Method, he pushed my arm and launched me backward. But the monk was a small elderly man, and there was probably a 15 cm height difference and a

20 kg weight difference between us. And he could barely even walk with his injured leg. The way that monk stood was the key for me to understand the Rubber Ball Power. When he pushed me, he didn't seem to tense his legs, arms, or anywhere else.

When you master the Rubber Ball Power, you'll realize that it's not a result of muscle strength from any one part of your body. Instead, you'll see that it's a method of using your body in which each body part works together closely to transmit your weight onto your opponent. That's why the monk didn't seem to use any one part of his body or muscle strength.

While power is said to come from the legs or the ground, you don't even need to step hard on the ground. If you were to generate power by stepping hard on the ground, it wouldn't be from your weight or the ground—it would be muscle strength from your legs.

While a rubber ball has the elasticity to rebound when pushed, it doesn't expand on its own. When you fully express the Rubber Ball Power, there is almost no sense of exertion in any one part of your body. This is like how the elasticity of a rubber ball is created throughout the ball, not just at the point of contact. And you can only feel the rubber ball's elasticity because the ball is touching the ground.

When you land a clean punch, there's a surprising lack of tension in any specific body part, and it feels effortless. You don't feel like you've stepped hard on the ground, and you don't feel any tension in your back. This is a result of power from the ground being transferred to your opponent without being interrupted anywhere in your body. You have unleashed **the Rubber Ball Power perfectly. The Rubber Ball Power is about making your body the intermediate route (intermediary)**

between the ground and your opponent.

But just because there's no sense of exertion, it doesn't mean muscle strength is unnecessary. Your entire structure and muscle strength came together like a rubber ball to transmit force to your opponent. So, of course, the stronger your muscles, the better. **I'd like to emphasize that the Rubber Ball Power isn't dismissing muscle strength or forms—it's addressing a different layer.**

Move the Parts That Aren't Touching Your Opponent

When you want to control your opponent, you'll try to move them according to your will. To move your opponent, you'll try to move the point of contact between you and your opponent. And if your hands are in contact with your opponent, you'll try to move your arms to push, pull, and hit your opponent.

The Tripod Method takes the opposite approach. **It is about maintaining your power and posture by minimizing movement at the point of contact with your opponent while moving the other areas.**

A rubber ball caves in where it's pressed. It yields to pressure. But the internal air pressure prevents it from caving past a certain point. And this pressure is not only created where you push the ball but by the tension of the entire ball. The same is true in the Tripod Method, which develops the Rubber Ball Power. The parts of your body that aren't under pressure move and generate more power than those that are. If you've read this far, you probably already know that I'm not suggesting that there's air or "qi" pressure in your body. While you're moving like a rubber ball, the source of your power is the strength of your muscles, bones, and other structures.

In the Front Push exercise I've introduced for example, there's little need to force any movement at the point of contact. You just need to continue adapting your entire body, with your hips at the center, in a way that makes you strongest against the direction of your opponent's pressure. And, while the arms may move, you'll miss the point of this exercise if you only look at the arms and try to analyze their positions, as this would make it about strength.

Motionless Power, Unmoving Power

The Rubber Ball Power is the ability to balance. And, because it's the ability to not just lean in one direction, you can also feel it as **the ability to stay in place.**

Sports and martial arts trainings are primarily concerned with how to move. They are about moving as forcefully, quickly, and precisely as possible. But the Rubber Ball Power develops stability and the ability to remain still. While it can be used to push your opponent, it creates a body that absorbs your opponent's force and keeps you from being pushed, with the ground ultimately absorbing this force. When you push a ball into the ground, it absorbs your force and transfers it to the ground—this is the same. **You could call it a passive power that**

grounds your opponent's force.

It's the ability to push while you pull—a contradictory power. It's the ability to push and pull your opponent simultaneously, to thrust your head up while sinking down, and to push and pull a wall on your right side while simultaneously pushing and pulling a wall on your left side.

Both agility and reflexes decline with age. On the other hand, power doesn't necessarily decline with age. Finding a lightweight champion in their forties would be difficult in boxing, but heavyweight George Foreman became a champion at 45.

If you want to continue your martial arts training beyond your so-called physical peak, it's crucial to develop both speed and a form of power that doesn't deteriorate. The source of the Rubber Ball Power cultivated through the Tripod Method is weight, that is, body weight. This isn't something that declines with age. While some people unfortunately gain weight by putting on excess fat, even this is converted into power.

Of course, you won't win competitions without moving correctly. There's no doubt, however, that being able to move while maintaining this "power of immobility" or being able to activate this power at any time, will boost your competitiveness. In fact, all skilled athletes in various sports should have a highly developed ability similar to the Rubber Ball Power.

An Innate Ability Taken for Granted

The Tripod Method is simple. What it conveys is summed up as the "Rubber Ball Power," and this power is something that every human possesses.

Most people can understand, experience, and learn it in a 90-minute session. And I hear two types of responses when I talk to those who have acquired the Rubber Ball Power in such a session. The first, "This is incredible!" and the other, "Oh, isn't this obvious?" Both reactions make me very happy. Yes, this is obvious. No one would be surprised if they were taught how to breathe. That's because it comes naturally to everyone.

Like breathing, the Rubber Ball Power (balance) is something that we innately possess, making it an obvious ability. However, the most important abilities are those that we take for granted. Everyone has them because they are necessary for survival. While incredible abilities that only a few can acquire through years of training may be required for certain professions or lifestyles, they are not universal abilities that everyone needs.

And although I use the names "Tripod Method" and "Rubber Ball Power," it's nothing more than an ability that everyone uses daily without a second thought. But even if it's an ability that everyone has, it's not necessarily used at a high level. And because this ability is so commonplace, people who use it well are often assumed to have some natural sense and are considered "talented" or "athletic." But by naming it and focusing on it through exercises, anyone can experience and nurture this fundamental ability. **Truly amazing and important abilities are obvious, and everyone has them naturally without any training.**

Use Your Arms Like Your Legs, and Your Legs Like Your Arms

When you learn the Tripod Method and express the Rubber Ball Power in your arms, they will be powerful, as if they were your legs. And you'll find it easier than ever to withstand being pushed. Why is this the case?

The primary role of your arms is to control things. It includes lifting and moving objects, using tools, and pushing and pulling your opponent. Our hands have evolved in this way. That's why when we contact an opponent in sports and martial arts, we try to move them by pushing and pulling them with our arms.

On the other hand, the primary role of your legs is to support yourself. They work to maintain your balance and allow you to keep standing. Furthermore, your hips, knees, and ankles—all the joints in your legs—work to maintain your posture. We can hike up steep, unpaved mountain paths without considering the angles of our knees or ankles. This is an incredibly complex movement if you think about it. You are supporting your body, which weighs tens of kilograms, with only the tiny surface area of your feet, as you absorb each shock and move smoothly.

Humans becoming bipedal and clearly distinguishing the roles of our front legs (arms) and hind legs (legs) was a significant factor in our exceptional evolution. But something has become neglected as a result—**the sense of moving ourselves using our arms.**

As I mentioned earlier, there's an awareness that the arms move things while the legs move you. This isn't something within your conscious awareness that you can actively control. It's rooted in a deeper part of our consciousness known as the subconscious mind. Therefore, the body naturally and automatically reacts this way. When contacting an opponent in sports or martial arts, we try to push and pull them at the point of contact.

But there's an exception. It's when we contact something heavier than us that doesn't move. Nobody would put their hands on a wall expecting to move it. In this case, the sense of pushing the wall to move ourselves with the rebound arises naturally. It's also very natural in sports to move yourself via the point of contact between you and your opponent if they are heavier and stronger than you.

Supporting and moving yourself with your arms at their points of contact, rather than using them to move your opponent, is a leg-like way to use your arms. This is something ordinary that everyone naturally does, depending on the circumstances. Therefore, it isn't a sense that was lost completely.

The problem is, however, that since the arms are mainly used to move things, we often use them to try and move our opponents, even when they are heavier and stronger than us. That said, in sports, there are plenty of situations where you must push and move an opponent, no matter how much stronger they are. What can you do in such cases?

Reverse how you use your arms and legs. In other words, use your legs to move your opponent and arms to support yourself. **Use your**

arms in a leg-like way and your legs in an arm-like way. When pushing your opponent, use your arms primarily to support yourself rather than to push your opponent. And to move your opponent, leave that up to your legs and lower body, which are far stronger than your arms.

When colliding with your opponent, such as in rugby or sumo wrestling, you should also push them with your lower body rather than your arms. If your hips remain back in a so-called heppirigoshi, you're trying to push your opponent with your arms.

Using your legs in an arm-like way, that is, using them to move a subject (an opponent), is not a difficult sense to grasp. That's because it's a sense that's commonly used. For example, if you push someone while folding your arms, making them unusable, you will naturally push them with your body. The same is true in Oshikura Manju, a Japanese game where three or more players stand back-to-back in a circle and shove each other with their backs.

On the other hand, we don't often use our arms in a leg-like way, to support and move ourselves. Additionally, our arms are far more dexterous than our legs. As a result, we tend to try and move our opponents with our arms.

Here, I'll introduce an easy exercise to use your arms in a leg-like way.

① **Place both palms and feet on the ground in front of a wall, standing on all fours.** <Figure 4-2>
In this posture, experiment with bending and

straightening your arms and legs and moving your head up, down, forward, and backward.

This is how it feels to support your body with your arms. Even when your posture changes, your body naturally balances itself.

Take yourself back to the quadrupedal days that are dormant within you.

② Place both palms towards the bottom of the wall and slowly climb up. <Figure 4-3>

③ Stand up straight with your palms touching the wall.

We gradually climb up the wall so that we can **stand up while maintaining how we felt on all fours.** You're doing well if you can preserve the sensation of touching the ground, even when standing straight with your arms perpendicular to the wall. It's like when a dog places its front legs on a table and stands up.

When your arms learn to support your weight like your legs, you will not overreact when you're pushed. When you step on a large pebble while hiking, you wouldn't try to stamp it into the ground because it's in your way. It doesn't matter if the path is uneven as long as you maintain your balance. **Your legs don't fight the ground.** In the same way, if your opponent pushes you, your arms should naturally pull back while you maintain your balance. **If you can use your arms in a leg-like way, instead of just pulling back lightly, you could also put your weight on your opponent's arm and pull back with power.**

What we're doing here, such as pulling your arms when they're pushed and pushing with your lower body, is nothing new. But using

<Figure 4-2>

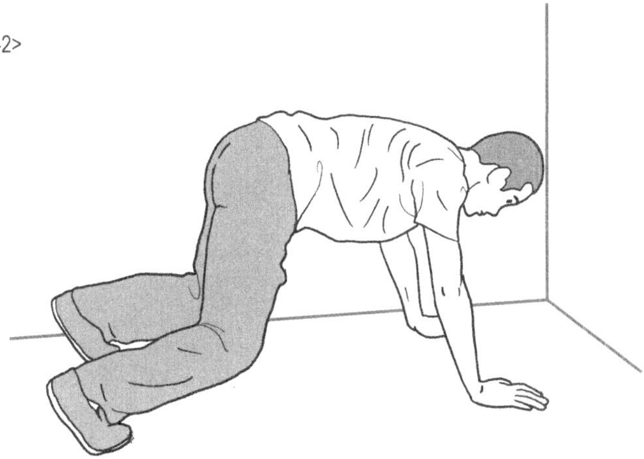

<Figure 4-3>

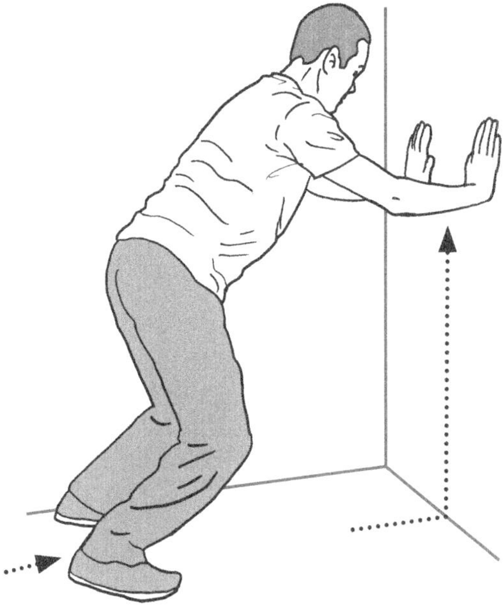

Stand on all fours with both hands and feet, and slowly walk up a wall with both hands. Continue to feel as if the wall were the ground. Keep this same sensation when you come into contact with another person.

your arms in a leg-like way will make a massive difference in your performance.

In reality, there is no difference between moving your opponent and moving yourself, and the expressions "using your arms in a leg-like way" and "using your legs in an arm-like way" are not perfect. **You are simply creating a structure in which your entire body is resisting an external force while maintaining its balance, with each part exerting itself proportionately to its strength.** I hope you enjoy this experience and the changes in the quality of your movements.

Chapter 5

Using Your Mind to Harness the Power of Your Body

Correlation Between Physical Sensation and Awareness

There's a theory that the Japanese word for "to learn," manabu, is derived from manebu, which means "to imitate."

In Qigong, we imitate nature. For example, by imitating the bold movements of a tiger or bear, we capture its bold energy in our bodies. Ritsuzen is also a form of Qigong. It's called Zhan Zhuang in China, and it's said to be an imitation of a tree. By standing quietly like a massive tree, we imitate its serenity and unshakable strength.

It's not entirely unscientific to imitate something to become like it. Being around irritable people will make you more irritable, whereas being around relaxed people will put you at ease. Additionally, you'll feel grim if you furrow your eyebrows, whereas your mood will lift if you keep smiling. In the same way, if you maintain a good posture, your mind will also start to clear. Feeling physically unwell when you're worried shows the impact of your mind on your body, while becoming somewhat cranky when you catch a cold shows the impact of your body on your mind. The mind and body are inseparable.

The brain, one of the body's organs, is the source of consciousness. In other words, we could say that consciousness and the body are two inseparable entities. They are one. Therefore, if we approach things from both the consciousness and physical perspectives, we should be able to create the most change.

Philosopher Kiyoshi Miki writes in his book: "Exercise is the control of correct judgment over the body's movements, and through it, the disorder of the mind can also be regulated. It is essential to know how to correctly exercise the body, which is being subjected to the whims of sentiments, in order to control the mind."

The significance of learning martial arts can also be found here. **If your body is a certain way, your mind will also be that way.** If you put your body in order, your mind will naturally be more inclined to order.

The same is true for the Tripod Method. I don't want to limit the Rubber Ball Power to just the physical level; I also want to expand it to the conscious level. The Rubber Ball Power is ultimately balance. This means **your consciousness will also naturally adjust toward balance.** Physical experiences affect our consciousness.

The Rubber Ball Power radiates in all directions while also concentrating at your center. It feels like you're being suspended and pulled from the top of your head while also pushing up the ceiling. It's a power that stretches your limbs while simultaneously concentrating at your center. This brings about a sense of fullness in your limbs as if they were filled with qi, so to speak. Energy flows where your attention goes. This may be difficult to imagine, but **my body feels as if it's unwinding and as if it's smiling gently.**

In Japan, it has long been recognized that developing a physical sense of your center, such as your axis or dantian, creates a psychological center.

A book by Katsu Kaishu, a Japanese national hero during the Bakumatsu period, mentions the following:

"Zazen and Kenjutsu served as my foundation, greatly benefiting me in my later years. Throughout the shogunate's dissolution, I have repeatedly escaped death and, eventually, lived out my life entirely due to the merits of these two. There was a time when numerous skilled swordsmen and others were out to get me, but I always came out on top. These two things ultimately nourished my courage and grit. When I faced a threat that I judged as inescapable, I immediately charged forward with everything on the line; and strangely, I never died. This demonstrates a tremendous psychological benefit at work."

A free body and mind that, while having a center, have no fixed direction.

Don't you think learning martial arts in a safe country like Japan would be more about mental rather than physical protection?

Don't Cling to the "Correct Forms" of a School

Every sport or martial art has its unique forms.

In Chinese martial arts, the chest is held gently rather than puffed out, and the pelvis is tilted slightly backward.

When tilting your pelvis and hips like this, you increase stability and passive strength but also limit your range of motion. On the other hand, a strong anterior pelvic tilt, like in elite track athletes, allows for agility by increasing the strength and range of motion around the gluteal muscles. When you puff your chest out and draw your belly in, your center of gravity rises to your chest, which increases your mobility. Conversely, when you puff your belly out, your center of gravity drops there, increasing your stability.

It's not about which is better. You must decide based on a sport's applications and characteristics.

You shouldn't become too attached to your style to the point of clinging to it. The forms and movements said to be "correct" in that style are merely a result of its founder selecting a small portion of universal human movements according to their ideas and physical tendencies.

Dismissing the movements and ideas of other styles as "wrong" is an attitude that fails to consider a multifaceted reality. The only thing that can truly be considered "correct" are the laws of nature, not someone's words or movements. Some postures are appropriate for those who have lost a leg in an accident, while others are appropriate for those who are crushed after losing a loved one. **True reality is free of human biases about "how things should be."**

If the Tripod Method had to prescribe a "correct form," it would be "a structure in accordance with the laws of nature." The laws of nature include the pressure created when you contact an opponent, centrifugal force, acceleration, friction with the ground when moving, and so on. So, in other words, the "correct form" would be to maintain a "structure that is in accordance with gravity." What we seek through the Tripod Method is "being" rather than "doing."

Ball of Qi (Qi Sensation)

In Ritsuzen, your fingertips will start to tingle. You will begin to feel a sensation in your arms as if you were hugging a ball—a sense of resistance as if the ball were elastic or magnetic. These sensations are sometimes called qi sensations in Qigong, but is this really the case?

When you experience the tingling in your fingertips, you'll understand that it's nothing mysterious. It's the same feeling you get when you enter a hot bath with a cold body and your blood flow increases. While the Ritsuzen won't significantly raise your heart rate, your body will warm up and you will sweat lightly. Most people will likely experience improved blood flow when trying it out.

There's a sense that Ritsuzen positively affects your mind and body, similar to how you'd feel when relaxing in a hot spring. In my case, I particularly feel the back of my head, temples, and the area between my eyebrows unwind, as well as a load off my chest. It feels more like your body unwinding first and your mind following rather than vice versa. While the back of my head and area between my brows don't usually feel so tight, you'll realize how tense you usually are when you experience true relaxation.

These sensations are lovely and will reset your mind and body to a neutral state. The sensation of the ball in your arms, on the other hand, isn't something you'll likely experience day-to-day. By imagining a ball (of energy) in the space within your arms, you'll feel an elasticity in your arms as if the ball were really there. When I first started practicing Ritsuzen, I thought this was just in my head. But it felt too real. The cause of this sensation also became clear to me through my training. **The elasticity of the ball in your arms is actually the weight of your arms.** Many people might disagree with me when I make this conclusion. I would never dismiss the energy-like entity known as "qi" simply because it hasn't been proven scientifically. Personally, while my definition of qi does differ, I do believe it to be the source of all things.

However, the ball you feel in your arms doesn't need this mysterious energetic explanation.

Here's what I mean when I say the ball's elasticity is the weight of your arms. First, the physical entities known as your arms have a weight. While we constantly experience this weight, we often don't pay much attention to it. For example, when we lift a water bottle, we are only aware of the bottle's 500 grams. But subconsciously, we feel the several kilos of our arms plus the 500 grams from the bottle. Next, when we try to move an entity with weight to it, we feel resistance. When we move our arm, a weighted entity, there is always resistance, even if we don't usually notice it. Shaking your arm once or twice isn't challenging at all, but by the time you've shaken it 100 times, you'll likely feel your arm's weight together with some fatigue.

In Ritsuzen, we raise our arms in front of our bodies as if hugging a ball. When you continue to imagine a ball in this posture, the resistance created by the weight of your arms can be felt as the elasticity (resistance) of the ball. That is what I mean when I say the elasticity of the ball in your arms is the weight of your arms. That's why you feel this resistance both inside and outside your arms. In Taikiken, we have the expression "as if you were moving underwater," where you feel this resistance throughout your body. The arms, rich in nerve endings and highly sensitive, make it easy to feel this resistance. Thus, by first sensing the resistance of the ball, or, in other words, the weight of our arms in Ritsuzen, we can more easily learn to feel our weight throughout our bodies.

Asserting that the sensation of the ball in Ritsuzen isn't qi may disappoint those seeking mysticism in the practice. This understanding, however, has led me to feel even more potential in Ritsuzen. This is because the understanding that the ball-like resistance is the weight of your arms leads to:

- **Sensing your body more deeply.**
- **Developing the ability to use your weight.**
- **Recognizing that your body is a mass of energy.**

When you can feel the weight of your arms and body, or the resistance you didn't feel before, you can sense your body and center of gravity more deeply than before. And, as I've repeatedly stated, the source of power in the Tripod Method is your weight. So, being able to sense this weight more precisely allows you to use it more skillfully. Furthermore, if you understand that weight is power, or in other words, energy, you will understand, not through thinking but through your felt sense, that your body, which is weighted, is a mass of energy.

As an aside, rulers have settled in elevated places and built tall buildings since ancient times. One reason might be that when a person is in an elevated place, they subconsciously sense that they are holding "potential energy," or physically possessing a higher level of energy.

There are also Qigong performances where people are sent flying with no touch. While Taikiken is based on Qigong techniques, we don't have techniques that send people flying without contact. Even if there were such no-touch techniques in other schools (which I'd gladly put to the test), they are probably not some amplified versions of the ball's elasticity felt during Ritsuzen.

Subjective and Objective: The Two Sides of Power

Power is bidirectional. If you push forward, there will always be a backward force. **When you understand the bidirectional nature of power and apply it to how you use your body, your explosive power and speed will increase, and you will gain the freedom to shift in any direction.**

Mentally, the bidirectionality of power can be explained through subjectivity and objectivity, as well as activity and passivity; physically, it can be explained through the law of action and reaction. And this power can be felt, developed, and strengthened primarily through Ritsuzen.

Ritsuzen has many ancient teachings about posture and awareness. "As if your head were suspended, as if your head were pushed down" is one of them.

Imagine standing upright and your head being pulled up by a rope attached to the crown of your head. The imagination here is more like a feeling or sensation than a mental image. You could say that you're imagining realistically with bodily sensations. You will then feel stretching in your neck, spine, hips, and knees. But you will not start floating in the air. This is because your body weight is pulling you down.

Conversely, imagine a giant pushing down on your head from above. Your neck, spine, and knees will feel compressed and start to bend. But you will not be crushed because your bones and muscles support you. **"Your head being suspended" is a sensation of being pulled up by**

an external force, whereas "your head being pushed down" is a sensation of being compressed down by an external force. However, these opposing forces are, in fact, the same thing. That's what "power is bidirectional" means.

Let's go back to the image of being suspended. The rope attached to the crown of your head is pulling you up. This image (sensation) actually contains another image: you pulling the rope down. You are suspended from above, and your body (body weight) is resisting by pulling down. "Being suspended" is an image where the upward force is passive, whereas "pulling down" is an active image where you exert the downward force.

What about the image of being pushed down? There is also another side to this sensation. "Being pushed down from above" includes the opposite sensation of pushing up from below. You are pushed down from above, so you are resisting to avoid being crushed. In this case, "being pushed down from above" is a passive image where your main focus is on the downward force, whereas "resisting by pushing up" is an active image where you exert the upward force.

Looking at it this way, you can see that "being suspended" or "being pushed down" is merely a difference in awareness, where you hold an active or passive awareness of either the upward or downward force. **In other words, "being suspended" and "being pushed down" both contain an upward and downward force, with the only difference being which force you feel more actively.**

These forces are always at work, even when we're just casually standing. But because the upward and downward forces are equal and cancel each other out, your body will not feel them without these images. However, when you can perceive these opposing, contradictory forces as they are, in contradiction, without canceling them out, you gain some abilities. They are, as I mentioned at the outset, "explosive power and speed" and the "freedom to shift in any direction."

I first want to use an example to explain why explosive power and speed are created. In Japan, we have a game called Dekopin, where you flick your index finger by creating a stopper with your thumb. If you try to flick your index finger without using your thumb as a stopper, you'll notice almost no power or speed. When your thumb stops your index finger from moving, the muscles of your index finger accumulate energy like a spring. The principle behind this and the upward and downward directions in the body I've just discussed are the same. Because you're suspended from above, you can rip that rope and drop down with speed and power. Because you're pushed down from above, you can burst through and rise with speed and power. Here, you might question that while the thumb is there as a resistance in the Dekopin, being suspended and pushed down are just imaginations. However, your body has a weight and a skeletal structure that supports it. These physical elements offer the resistance that corresponds to the thumb in the Dekopin, and the images are simply there as an aid. The downward force is gravity, and the upward force is the reaction to gravity created by your skeletal structure and muscles. Therefore, these forces are not a delusion or imagination. **When you keep the opposing forces in your body, you generate a strong and fast force when you break through them.**

Next is the freedom to shift in any direction. Here, I will use archery as an example. You nock an arrow on a bowstring and draw it back. When you let the arrow go, it will fly forward. This is also the same principle as the Dekopin, where a backward force becomes a forward force. You'd never do this in real life, but what if, after drawing back the arrow, you let go of the bow instead? The bow would fly back into your face, and you'd likely get injured. When you nock an arrow and draw it back, you simultaneously create the power to shoot the arrow forward and the power to make the bow fly backward. Returning to the upward and downward forces in your body, whether you're being suspended or pushed down from above, you're simultaneously storing upward and downward forces in both cases. When you cut the rope from above, you create an explosive downward force; when the ceiling above you disappears, you create an upward force.

In Ritsuzen, we primarily focus on these vertical forces while feeling the same resistance in the front, back, left, and right directions. By honing these sensations, you are developing an awareness and body that can move up, down, front, back, left, and right—in any of these directions. While you're trying to create a force in one direction in Dekopin and archery, they contain the potential for movement in the opposite direction. **This sense of stored power is one of the things you can acquire through Ritsuzen.** Your whole body will feel like a drawn bow. But this sensation doesn't mean you're tensing your body. The drawing power doesn't come from your muscles but from your mind and body weight. Therefore, you must feel your body weight. And you must be relaxed to feel your body weight. **When you tense up, the confounding factor of muscle strength makes it more difficult to perceive gravity.** Of course, you need muscle strength in the right direction to generate even more power. But it's essential to understand through Ritsuzen, that this power, which is primarily from your weight,

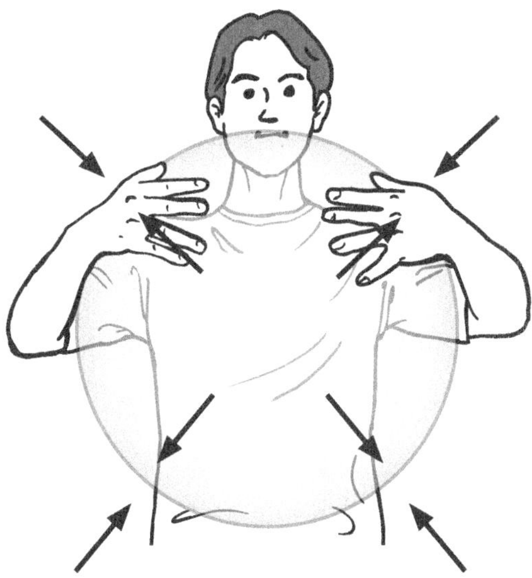

<Figure 5-1> Imagine hugging a ball in Ritsuzen. Pay attention to the bidirectional nature of power in this situation, where you are exerting inward pressure on the ball while the ball expands outward.

structure, and the elasticity of your muscles, feels slightly different from what we call muscle strength.

Power is always bidirectional, and your awareness is also relative. What about your arms holding the ball in Ritsuzen? When practicing Ritsuzen, you, the subject, are trying to hold the ball, so your arms exert power inwards toward the direction of compressing the ball. **<Figure 5-1>** But this ball is an imagination. If you try to feel this situation from the perspective of the ball, which can be called the object, it is being pushed by you and is resisting by expanding. From your perspective, your arms move inward, whereas your arms move outward from the ball's perspective.

For the "I'm holding the ball" image, there is the "ball being held by me" image on the other side. And in that moment, there's a real sense of resistance in your arms. As I explained earlier, this resistance isn't a sensation of qi but the weight of your arms. This weight plays the role of a stopper, like your thumb in Dekopin, and by momentarily releasing it outside or inside, you will create explosive power and speed, as well as a diversity of movement that can be expressed internally and externally.

In Ritsuzen, this feeling isn't just created in the arms but throughout the body. For example, it would feel like this for the legs. While in Ritsuzen, imagine you were about to jump. Because your hips aren't lowered deeply, you'd jump about 5 cm on the spot. But with your knees bent and hips lowered, you're in a state where you could jump immediately on cue. Let's observe this moment. Isn't this state, where your body is about to jump, the same as when you have just landed from a jump? **Your body is doing the same thing when you kick the ground to jump or support your weight upon landing.** It's merely your awareness deciding whether you're jumping or landing.

Consider a video of someone throwing a ball. The thrown ball would follow a parabolic path to the ground. If you played this video in reverse, the ball would follow the same curved trajectory from the ground back to your hand. Even in reverse, the same laws of physics are at work.

Whether you think you're jumping or landing, your body can initially move in either direction. **But once you fix your awareness, you can only move in that direction. Leaving the contradictory sensations that are there before you fix the direction of your awareness,**

without integrating them, is an awareness and experience you can find in Ritsuzen. A free awareness and body without a fixed direction.

Feeling your weight creates a sense of resistance. Heavy things are hard to move. This is obvious. **This resistance acts as a barrier to movement and produces power in two directions: one that breaks through the resistance and one that opposes this power.** There is freedom because there is restriction. Resistance allows you to generate a greater force. When you push a wall, a force exists between your hands and the wall, even though you're still. And this force both goes through the wall and pushes back against you. **There is freedom (movement) because there is restriction (resistance).**

Holding bidirectional power in your body means simultaneously expanding and contracting, very subtly, preferably within your awareness only. You contract your triceps to extend your elbows. You contract your biceps to bend your elbows. Like this, your body has antagonist muscles, and it's as if you're sending a very faint signal to every muscle in your body to fire. That's why Ritsuzen activates your entire body. Where the mind goes, power follows. When doing this, rather than pushing down hard on the ball or spring or imagining them too realistically, a subtle imagination and gentle sensation is better as it avoids unnecessary tension.

Expansion and Contraction/Diffusion and Concentration

Suspended from and pushed down on the crown of your head, bending and extending your entire body. You can summarize these sensations as the expansion and contraction of your mind and body. When doing Ritsuzen, the body feels as if it's expanding. Like a balloon, there is pressure from the inside out. This, too, isn't a delusion where your imagination has altered your perception. Instead, it's a sensation that arises from subtly pushing up, down, forward, backward, left, and right.

Expanding means the skin on the front of your body, including your chest and abdomen, feels a forward force. What about 1 or 2 cm deep (inside the body) from the surface of your chest and abdomen? As you go deeper, you'll notice that the forward force becomes a force toward your center the moment you go behind the center of your body. In other words, the forward force becomes a force in the direction of contraction. Conversely, while the back of your body feels a backward force during expansion, when you feel this force in the front of your body, you'll see that it also becomes a force toward your center, or a contractionary force. Therefore, **an expansionary force is a contractionary force, and vice versa.**

There are also many changes to your awareness during Ritsuzen. When you're standing in Ritsuzen, there are times when your awareness wanders to your breath. You observe your inhales and exhales without intentionally focusing on them, and your awareness gradually concentrates there. And as your concentration on the breath deepens,

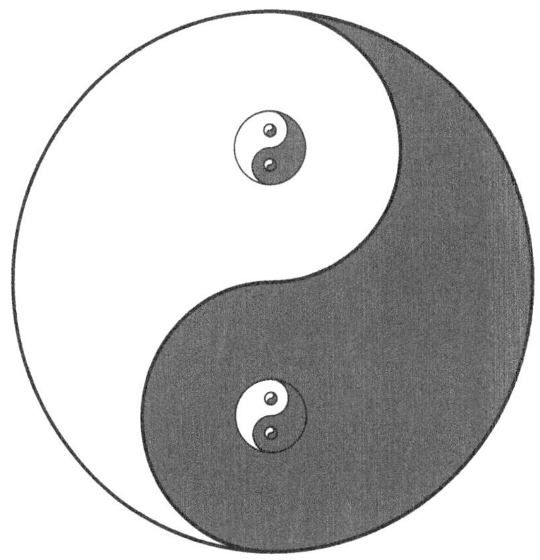

<Figure 5-2> In the Yin-Yang Taiji diagram, there is Yang within Yin and Yin within Yang. I sense that both Yin and Yang exist within these as well, forming an ever-unfolding fractal pattern.

you'll notice the in-breath passing through your nose and throat and entering your lungs, and the out-breath from your nose swirling and diffusing over your lip. You'll begin to notice things you haven't noticed before. While you were initially focused on only the inhale and exhale, **when your focus intensifies on a single point, your awareness expands throughout your body.**

Like this, **while expansion and contraction, concentration and diffusion appear to be opposed, each encompasses the opposite aspect in a Yin-Yang dynamic.**

By the way, are you familiar with the Yin-Yang Taiji diagram? **<Figure 5-2>** The dark color represents Yin, while the light color represents

Yang, and together they make Taiji (the Supreme Ultimate). Here, notice the small Yang inside the Yin (○), and the small Yin inside the Yang (●). While in Ritsuzen, you'll notice the nested structure of opposing entities, such as expansion and contraction, subjectivity and objectivity. Then, maybe this small Yin and Yang aren't just Yin and Yang but small Yin-Yang Taiji diagrams themselves, creating an infinitely unfolding fractal pattern. This is based on my intuition rather than a study of the literature, so it is not definitive.

Martial Arts Is Communication

The opponents that martial arts assume aren't bears or lions. They are humans.

Martial arts, in the first place, are systems of techniques for confronting humans with malicious intent and surviving such situations. Therefore, a martial art can't just be a system of physical movements, such as how to swing a pole or blade. Martial arts are a form of interpersonal communication.

The goal of communication is to look for common ground with the other person and to reach a mutual agreement. And the goal of martial arts is to survive a crisis. Given these assumptions, we must reconsider concepts such as "competition" and "winning or losing." Are martial arts really about winning? Is its purpose to deal a crushing blow to your opponent so you can soak in feelings of superiority and accomplishment?

There are levels to conflict. Initially, there's distance between two people and it begins with an argument, this then escalates to physical threats, a physical confrontation, and, eventually, killing each other. Where does it begin, and where does it end? Do you assume hostility from the start, or do you communicate peacefully?

Being the decision-maker here means setting rules to your advantage, and only when you include this layer will you truly find yourself unrivaled.

In a quarrel, you wouldn't suddenly break a beer bottle and stab the other person. You want to be the one to decide the level of conflict. What is your desired outcome? Do you want to force the other person to their knees, or do you want to end with a laugh and a handshake?

If your goal in a conversation is to win, you will try to outwit the other person in an argument or persuade them. An expert debater may win an argument, but this doesn't mean they have gained trust.

For me, the ideal outcome of a conflict is a draw and mutual recognition.

Even if I were stronger, I wouldn't utterly crush my opponent. The other person would resent you if you beat them to a pulp. If I were weaker, I would admit that and use it as motivation. When you remember to respect the other person, you create the opportunity for a mutually positive exchange.

When you hit someone, you become part of a causal system in which you'll also be hit. Isn't it necessary to break free from such a system?

We must avoid turning the means into an end. Beating someone up is a means, not an end.

What's your goal? You'll get lost if you don't set it properly.

Personally, my goal is mutual recognition and understanding. For that, a draw is better than a victory. Furthermore, your opponent's victory doesn't necessarily mean your loss, and vice versa.

To fight or not to fight.

You've already lost when you have no choice but to fight a stronger opponent.

Martial Arts to Enhance Homeostasis

I'd like to present "an improved homeostasis" as one of the goals of martial arts training. Homeostasis is when an organism survives by adapting to various environmental changes and maintaining constant internal conditions. Examples include the stability of blood composition and regulation of body temperature, and animals primarily accomplish this through nerves and hormones (According to the Daijirin).

The "strength" you can gain through Taikiken's Ritsuzen and other Qigong practices likely has an aspect of neurological and hormonal stability.

Have you ever heard about athletes having surprisingly vulnerable bodies? I've also trained in various sports, including combat sports, and felt more prone to getting sick than non-athletes. A body fatigued from training has a weakened immune system and is more susceptible to ailments—especially when cutting weight for bodybuilding and sports with weight limits.

Physical fitness can be divided into two categories: active fitness and defensive fitness. Active fitness refers to the physical ability to move and act. Defensive fitness refers to resistance and immunity against illness and stress and the ability to adapt to the environment. The vulnerable bodies of athletes mean people with excellent active fitness may not necessarily have excellent defensive fitness.

From a traditional martial arts perspective, having a strong body doesn't just mean being big, having muscle strength, and excelling at combat—it must also include qualities such as resistance to sickness, heat, and cold, as well as endurance. Without a starting bell, you never know when you might encounter a dangerous situation—and being sick won't work as an excuse.

Ritsuzen regulates neuronal activity through the mind. While you are more or less still in Ritsuzen, you start to sweat, and your muscles begin to fatigue. But your breath never quickens. **Ritsuzen is considered "exercise while resting."**

I often hear people say they no longer catch colds after having built a Ritsuzen practice, and this has also been my experience. Taikiken is also traditionally practiced outside rather than in a dojo, and being exposed to the elements, including the heat in the summer and cold in the winter, might be a training in and of itself.

While Ritsuzen is an excellent way to improve defensive fitness, I'd like to expand a bit on homeostasis. Homeostasis, in other words, is the maintenance of an environment. And martial arts, in general, is the art of protecting yourself from danger. Protecting your ordinary life from abnormal situations that we call danger—that is martial arts. Originally, the primary purpose of martial arts wasn't to attack aggressively but to keep yourself and surroundings normal and restore a disturbed balance.

Therefore, **martial arts can be considered a way to promote homeostasis and balance.**

Three Types of Shuai Shou and Their Axes

There's an exercise called Shuai Shou, where we swing our arms. It's a Qigong practice, but I will present it here as simply a physical exercise.

The Shuai Shou exercise I will introduce involves rotating your arms like a pellet drum. Stand with your feet shoulder-width apart and swing your arms from side to side, with the power coming from hip rotation. Your arms should be dangling and relaxed.

There are three variations, and I'd like you to try each one.

▶ Shuai Shou (Front) <Figure 5-3>

When your right arm comes forward, your right foot should stand on its toes. When your right arm wraps around the front of your body, your center of gravity should be on your left foot, toward your toes. Rotate with the force of extending up. Your center is behind the dantian, towards your back, and your belly draws an arc.

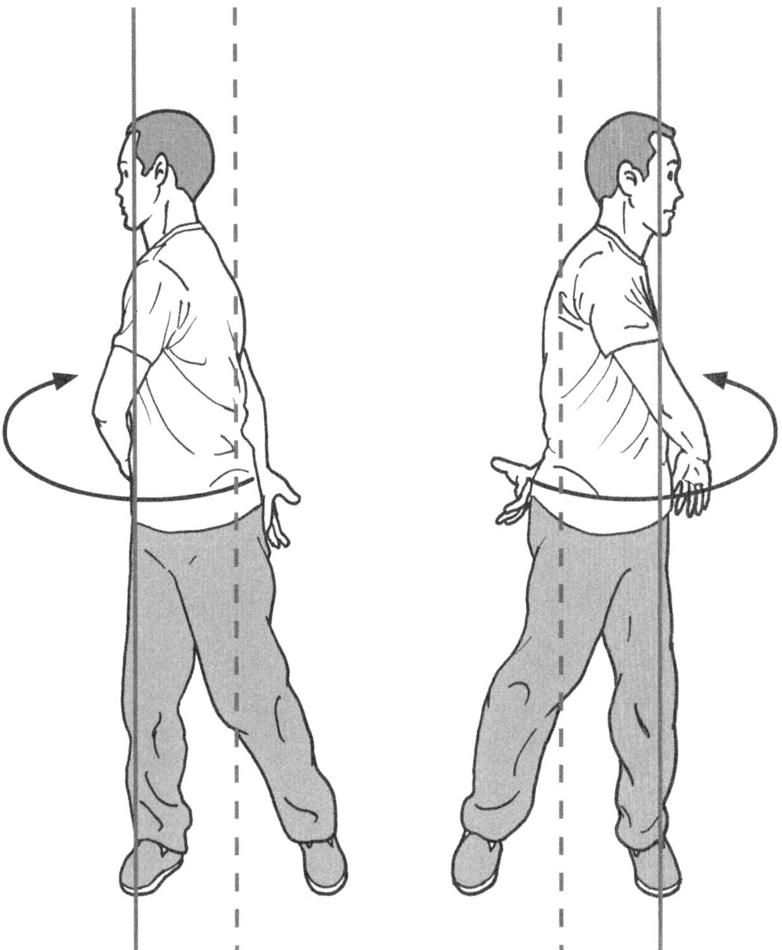

<Figure 5-3> The movement of Shuai Shou (Front). Rotate with the force of extending upward.

▶ Shuai Shou (Back) <Figure 5-4>

When your right arm comes forward, sink down on your right foot. When your right arm wraps around the front of your body, your center of gravity should be on your right foot, toward your heel. Rotate with the force of sinking down. Your center is in front of the dantian, towards your belly button, and your back and butt draw an arc.

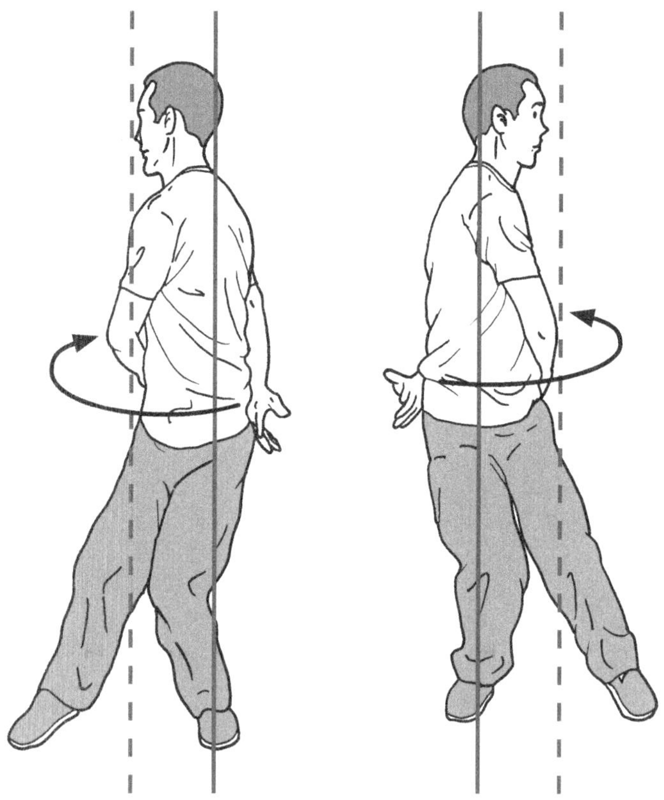

<Figure 5-4> The movement of Shuai Shou (Back). Rotate with the force of sinking down.

Shuai Shou (Center) <Figure 5-5>

We will combine Shuai Shou (Front) and Shuai Shou (Back). You will only rotate from your solar plexus up. Your feet and hips will be facing forward and still, but there will be a resistance with each rotation.

Start with the Front or Back variation, gradually minimize your movement, and eventually shift to the other variation. You should feel

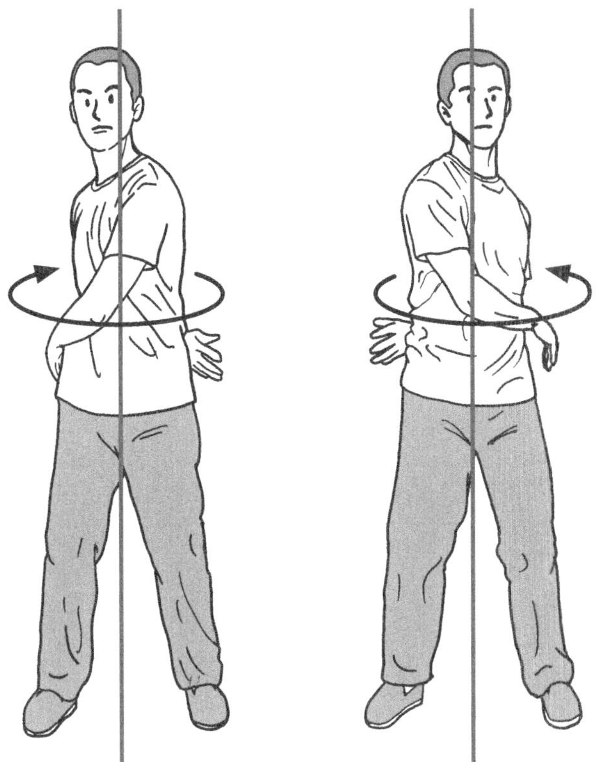

<Figure 5-5> The movement of Shuai Shou (Center). It is important to feel a combination of the forces in the aforementioned front and back variations.

the sensation of both variations in your body.

While the Center variation is what you ultimately want to practice, you'll be doing something with little movement or power if you don't practice the other variations. What's important is the combination of the Front and Back variations, with the power of each variation present, and you want to internally experience the power of your lower body and core without getting caught up with the external form.

Through these three Shuai Shou variations, I'd like you to confirm the following:

▶ The path of power

Focus on crossing the power in your body, with the power from your right arm originating in your left leg, and vice versa.

▶ The position of your axis

While feeling the path of power, you can also feel the position of your axis. Your pivot foot will be on the side opposite to your power arm.

▶ Movement and power

Larger movements don't necessarily mean more power. You can confirm this when you notice that you can generate the most power in the Center variation. While it's tempting to make big movements when you want to throw a powerful punch, there's another way.

I'd like to ask those practicing a striking art to check the following:

when you're in an orthodox stance, which leg generates power for your left fist (front fist), and which foot is your pivot foot? What about your right fist? You might think that your back leg (right leg) generates the power in both cases. If that were the case, aren't you using your body differently for your right and left fists?

You can also make the same investigation with a movement like the Udemawashi no Neri in Taikiken. **<Figure 5-6>**

The repetition of simple practices reveals the essence of human body movement more easily than complicated practices.

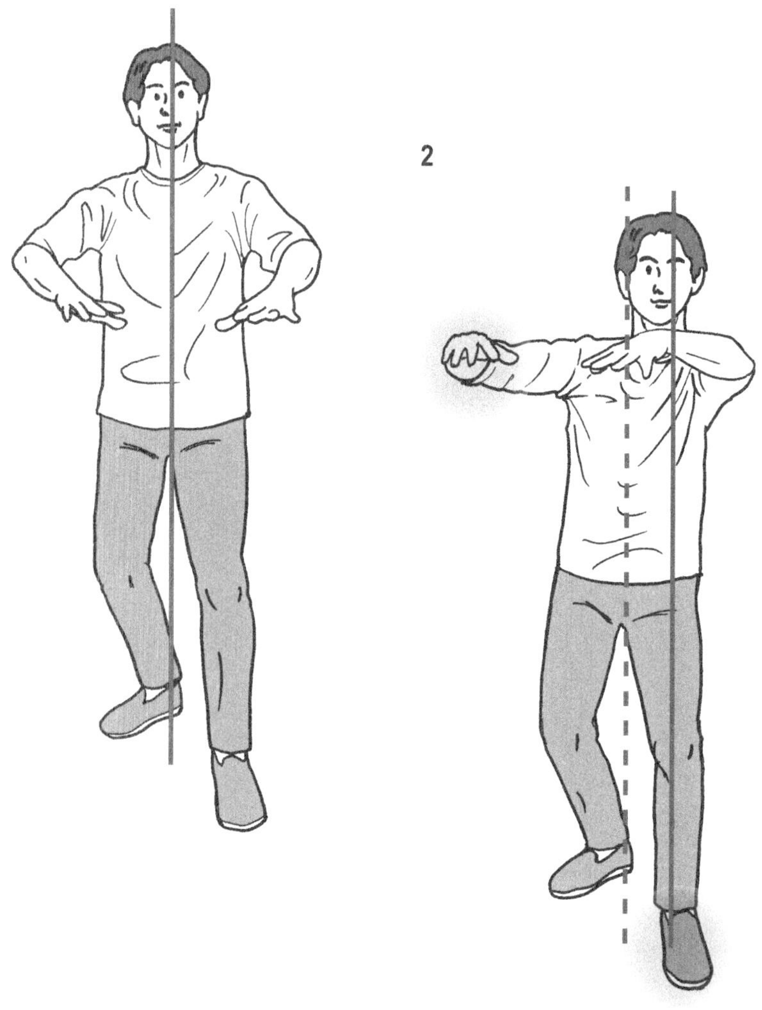

<Figure 5-6> An example of Neri, a fundamental movement in Taikiken. Feel the power of your left leg in your right hand and the power of your right leg in your left hand.

3

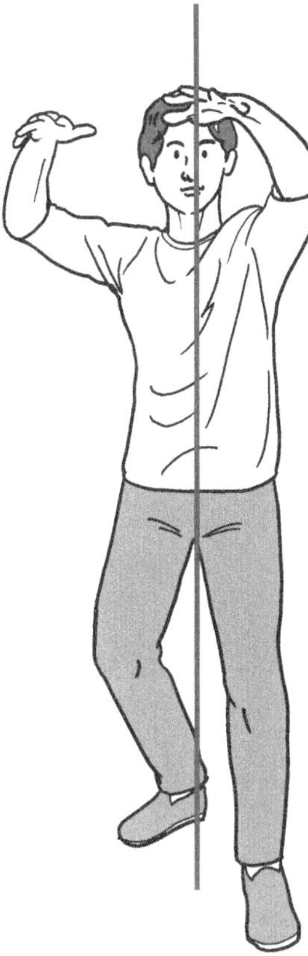

4

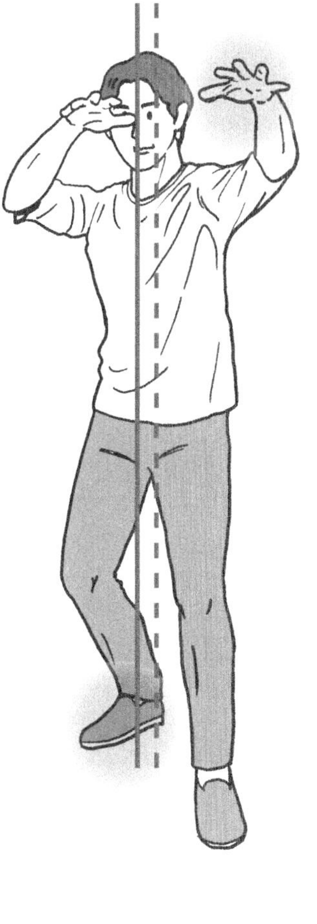

Relying on Many People

The Tripod Method improves your balance and enhances your ability to stand straight. The source of its power is gravity and leaning in all directions. And when you lean in all directions, you'll be "leaning without leaning," allowing you to stand independently and powerfully in balance.

Perhaps the same could also apply to our everyday lives. We want to allow ourselves to depend on others.

We often hear "Don't depend on others" or "Don't be a burden." However, humans, or any other living creature, can't survive without depending on something. Just having rice on our dining tables requires the help of many people, including farmers, transportation workers, and retailers. We must depend on roads, cars, subway systems—other people—to even get to work.

In today's highly developed and organized society, shouldn't we aim to depend on as many people as possible, instead of not depending on anyone?

Rather than reduce our sources of dependence, we must continue to increase them.

When we only depend on a few sources, we will fall if a source vanishes. A NEET who only depends on their parents would be in trouble if their parents pass away. It would also be hard for their parents. With a part-time job, however, they could get by. With a boyfriend or girlfriend, they could maybe share a place. With many friends, someone might find them a full-time job. A factory subcontracted by a large corporation also tends to be at the whims of that corporation, as a high percentage of their sales would come from it. One way to overcome this situation and increase security is to diversify their sales channels and reduce their reliance on that corporation.

Humans can't survive without burdening others. You'll become stuck if that's all you worry about. Because no matter what you do, you will always (supposedly) burden another person. Therefore, it's more realistic to increase the number of people you rely on while reducing your reliance on any one person.

In the investment world, there's also the saying "Don't put all your eggs in one basket." If you put all your eggs in one basket, dropping that basket would break all the eggs. It teaches us that instead of investing all our capital in one source, we can reduce our risk by diversifying our investments.

Instead of trying to live without burdening anyone, you'll become freer if you increase your tolerance for others' burdens as you also burden others—and thank those who help you.

Furthermore, since you rely on others, when others rely on you, meet their expectations to the best of your ability. **Relying on others makes life easier, and being relied on can make life more enjoyable.** You'll naturally begin to find your center as you rely on and are relied on.

Chapter 6

Lessons from Sparring

Sparring for Fun: Playful Sparring

When you look at an opponent, there's an opponent. When you look away, there's no opponent. You can't compare reality. In this book, **I've introduced the power of Ritsuzen from subjective and objective perspectives, but that was for convenience—just a transit point.** You can't compare things without the concepts of time and memory. To compare the "A" in front of you to the "B" you saw in the past, you must bring back the "B" in your mind. Therefore, **reality doesn't have contradictions.** When you look to the right, there's only what's to the right; when you look to the left, there's only what's to the left.

What is a "real fight"? When learning martial arts, we often hear phrases such as "In a real fight" and "For a real fight." To me, a "real fight" just means "reality." Your everyday life and daily practice—those are the real fights. For Japan's Self-Defense Forces, their day-to-day training is their real fight. This isn't because Japan has renounced war. The present moment doesn't exist to prepare for something—the present moment is all there is. When you're training, the training itself is reality—the real fight. When you're practicing, there's only that practice. When you're sparring, there's only that bout. However, interpreting this as a mental approach will distract us from reality again.

Perhaps the most important thing we can realize through martial arts and Ritsuzen is the nature of reality. Forms for punching and kicking, how to use your muscles, and where to place your awareness. There is no universal truth to any of this. While reality underlies all the opinions that differ between styles, you'll miss it if you only study the surface. Reality is what all the arts (including martial arts), as well as academic disciplines, sports, human activities, and everything else, have in common—and understanding it is the purpose of my martial arts training. This is something you can only seek within yourself in the present moment—not anywhere else.

Martial arts is communication. When confronting someone, we want to choose our goals and points of compromise. **My desired outcome for a confrontation is to build a relationship of mutual recognition in which we can laugh and shake hands.**

We do not compete in Taikiken. However, we frequently spar to put our training to the test. And because we don't have any competitions, there are no clear rules for sparring. We don't wear protective equipment, and pretty much anything goes except for ground fighting—that's about it. While palm strikes are the norm, that's also fuzzy, and there's even an atmosphere where people who get hit in their vitals are considered careless. Unsurprisingly, there are many injuries when sparring like this, and even if you wanted to fight all out, you must naturally consider each other's abilities and conditions. I used to believe that setting clearer rules and creating a competition-style environment where we could fight hard while taking safety precautions was more practical and effective.

Currently, however, I enjoy the ambiguity. **It's precisely this ambiguity that allows you to learn the most important lesson, which is to choose your points of compromise.** What's the other person's ability? What do they think about me? Is my school's or style's reputation on the line? Many thoughts cross each person's mind.

And my point of compromise is to build a relationship of mutual recognition in which we can laugh and shake hands. There's the saying to "eat from the same pot," but sparring builds camaraderie just as well as eating together does. **We all like to play superhero and WWE. Sparring, at the end of the day, is just playing—an unnecessary game.** Instead of calling it a study of techniques, a simulation of a fight, or mental training, just have fun.

As the Analects of Confucius states, "One who knows is no match for one who likes. One who likes is no match for one who enjoys." **Having fun brings people together.** As you spar, you'll feel if the other person wants to beat you up, if they're having fun, how hard they're hitting, and so on. Deal with your opponent as you feel these things. When you enjoy sparring, you'll naturally want to improve and will study. While our practices at the Buzenkai don't involve hitting punching bags and so on, our members do so on their own. When you grow fond of something, you'll be motivated to practice. The pine tree and plum tree are both beautiful in their own right.

The real reason I practice martial arts isn't to protect myself or for self-development. I just enjoy it. And I enjoy sparring and training with people who enjoy the same thing. **Sparring and training to win in competitions is wonderful. But winning isn't all there is to communication.** And training for a match is always training to win. Before making my living from martial arts, I was an office worker and also experienced running my own company. And in business, I learned that **society isn't a world of winning or losing.** When selling something, bonding with customers over understanding their needs is a more successful approach than having an attitude of competing against other companies. And if you survive as a result, people might say you've beat your competition. But that's just the outcome.

Sparring should be fun. Treat it as play and take it easy. And spar in a way that minimizes injury for you and the other person; and in a way that strengthens friendships once it's over. That is how we spar at the Buzenkai.

Developing Quickness Instead of Speed

As we age, our agility and reflexes reduce noticeably. What becomes necessary, then, is the ability to read indications. It is not about reacting quickly after your opponent has moved but about sensing their movements at an earlier stage and responding to them.

Being quick comes from sensitivity, thoroughness, and experience—not reflexes.

Speed is the relationship between time and distance. Moving 50 cm in 3 seconds is faster than moving 1 m in 10 seconds. And you must improve your reflexes to go from perceiving one second in two parts to perceiving it in three.

However, perceiving one centimeter in finer divisions comes down to more than just reflexes. Just as a chef can accurately add seasonings and a carpenter can cut wood into precise measurements by eye, experience and practice are undeniably at play. Likewise, your ability to read your opponent's next moves from subtle eye or shoulder movements improves rather than declines with age.

For example, in a striking martial art, you will begin to sense your opponents' "attacking intent" with practice. You'll come to sense when your opponent is about to attack from their overall atmosphere.

For instance, they may move their shoulder, pull back their hand, shift their legs, and so on. But more than anywhere else, it shows up in the eyes. Whether their pupils dilate or their gaze shifts, the eyes are first to change when we move. Sensing this comes down to your ability to observe your opponent together with your collection of past data. In other words, your experience plays a significant role.

The ability to accurately perceive "amount of change" could be considered a factor that increases speed.

Focus is another important factor for speed. After thousands of rounds of sparring, you'll realize that no matter who your opponent, no one can maintain their focus on their opponent for the entire bout. There are always moments when your opponents' attention wavers. When you notice the gaps in your awareness, such as when you blink, you can detect these gaps in your opponents and strike during them. After the age of 30, we want to hone our sensitivity and thoroughness rather than rely solely on our reflexes.

There Is No Distinction Between Offense and Defense

When I first began my Taikiken training, I was perplexed by something very different from the combat sports and martial arts I had previously practiced. We were rarely taught how to attack or defend ourselves during practice. Taikiken does incorporate free sparring into its training, where we learn offensive and defensive strategies in an interpersonal context, such as "When they do this, do that." However, we don't practice basic skills like punching, kicking, and throwing on their own or get clear demonstrations of them.

The Taikiken equivalent for the movement practices of other styles is called Neri. It involves walking back and forth while continuously performing movements such as rotating the arms in front of the body or pushing the arms forward. And while the master occasionally gives an example of use, such as "That is sometimes used like this," such explanations merely provide an example of how a movement could be used. Nippon Kenpo, in contrast, is simple and clear-cut, with instructions such as "The straight left punch is only used to strike your opponent" and "The scooping block is only used when your opponent kicks." But Taikiken's Neri uses the same movement for a wide range of applications, such as a strike in some cases, a grappling-like technique to unbalance your opponent in other cases, or a defensive technique to evade punches.

I found this breadth of applications confusing and unclear when I first started training. However, I have come to understand that Taikiken's Neri isn't just for teaching offensive or defensive techniques. Of course, there's that side to it, but more important is **developing a body that can move while maintaining power.** If there is power in your arms when you rotate them in front of your body, it becomes an attack if it hits your opponent's face and a block if it hits your opponent's arm as they strike. **A significant difference between Neri and movements like punching, kicking, and blocking is that Neri exerts power over a broader range, both in distance and time.**

Typically, a punch or kick aims to exert the most force at its moment of impact with your opponent. When you punch, for example, if your fist is intercepted before your arm is extended, when your elbows are still bent, you probably won't be able to straighten your arm any further. That's because there's no power in that arm. A whip produces the greatest force at its tip during impact, but that force doesn't exist at its base. A well-performed Neri, on the other hand, maintains constant power. This is based on the idea that colliding with a heavy stone lantern would cause a significant force upon impact, even if the lantern is stationary. The theory is that if you move like a stone lantern, you can move while maintaining constant power, no matter where you're held down.

Of course, the problem is that if you don't move quickly enough, you'll never be able to strike your opponent. We, traditional martial artists, must resolve this dilemma by interacting with mixed martial artists, kickboxers, and the like.

Power that comes through movement is a so-called active form of power generated through methods such as stepping in and increasing the speed of hip rotation. In Taikiken's Neri, on the other hand, we also want to have a **passive form of power,** or the ability to remain still when pushed.

In reality, the distinction between attacking and defending isn't so clear, and everyone should naturally be striking defensively and receiving offensively.

When your body is defending, your mind must be on offense. Otherwise, your opponent will charge forward and attack relentlessly. When your body is attacking, your mind must be on defense. Otherwise, you will be surprised with a counter. A skilled General considers retreat while attacking and plans the counterattack while defending.

With Neri, we simply aim to maintain a powerful posture at all times without thinking about attacking or defending. **A powerful posture, in Taikiken, means the mind-body structure developed through Ritsuzen.** I introduced an aspect of that power in this book as the Tripod Method. The primary goal of Neri is to move while preserving the power you have developed in Ritsuzen. When you think, "This is for offense" or "This is for defense," you'll limit your movements to those purposes only. As the movements of Neri become ingrained in your body, you'll be able to use them naturally while sparring, allowing you to **just let your hands move.**

Attacking, defending, striking techniques, grappling techniques, and ground techniques—these things don't actually exist in combat. This becomes clear when you watch animals fight. Whether striking or biting, fleeing or chasing, **they just face that moment with all their might—a seamless event. The arms, the body—they move on their own.**

Strike Without Thinking

There is something called Mushin (a state of "no mind"). Of course, it's important to be strategic and use the right combinations when you fight. However, there are times when a spontaneous strike drops your opponent. It may even be more common to cleanly knock your opponent out in this way. And while we do get a taste of what it's like to strike in a state of Mushin in those moments, the "no-mindedness" makes for poor reproducibility. Does this lack of reproducibility make it a mere coincidence? Is there no way to practice this?

There was a time when I practiced archery. As a professional martial artist, I was drawn to the atmosphere of Kyudo, but I chose archery because I believed that its sole purpose of hitting the target, rather than focusing on posture and so on, would allow me to train my mind and body with a more objective set of standards. Hitting a target dozens of meters away with millimeter accuracy is an excellent way to sharpen your bodily awareness.

I was practicing with what are called compound bows. Unlike the simple recurve bows used in the Olympics, compound bows have upper and lower pulleys that reduce their draw weight while increasing their power and accuracy. As a result, compound bows are primarily used in modern bowhunting. You may also remember it as the bow used in the movie Rambo. On top of it being structurally more accurate than the bows used in the Olympics, the compound bow also has sights. You also wear a special tool on the finger drawing the bow, where you release the arrow by clicking its button like the trigger of a gun. This minimizes hand movement and further improves accuracy.

During my brief foray into archery, I had a fascinating experience shooting thousands of arrows with this bow. After learning the basics, I gradually began to understand how to angle my body and hand, the timing of release and so on, as I shot arrow after arrow. And I started experimenting with various improvements. When I release the arrow as the center of the target aligns with the center of the sight, the arrow shoots through the center of the target. This is obvious, as the bow is calibrated this way. But because the body can't be completely still, the center of the target moves constantly within the sights. My strategy here was to work with this movement and release the arrow before the center of the target aligned with the sights. As I continued to practice releasing the arrow at just the right moment, I began noticing my quirks.

One day, while shooting my arrows, I accidentally launched one in an absent-minded state. While I aimed at the target as usual, I haphazardly released the arrow before my aim was set. My blood ran cold as I realized the arrow was now entirely out of my control.

Arrows have killed people in fatal accidents. Of course, there was no such danger as I was aiming at the target, but the feeling was like accidentally dropping a kitchen knife on the floor. I may even have let out an "Oh!"

When I went to collect that arrow from the target, I was shocked once again. The arrow had pierced the target dead-center, unlike anything I had ever seen. **My body had released the arrow on its own at the perfect moment. It only felt like an accident because "I" had not shot the arrow.**

I've shot thousands of arrows since then, but the same thing has only happened three times. And each time, it's a spectacular bull's-eye.

This experience taught me about Mushin—that the body moves independently and can far exceed what is possible through conscious control.

When sparring, a spontaneous shot also usually drops your opponent. Perhaps the only way to master this is to put in the hours. In a fight, you can't knock your opponent out at will. It's up to your opponent whether or not they are knocked out. **All you can do is strike.**

Aiuchi: The Fundamental Yet Ultimate

You will never become a strong fighter if you only practice your techniques without any free sparring. There are many reasons for this, but a major one is not knowing the right timing to use the techniques. When sparring, there's a free-moving opponent. Sparring demands an intuitive sense that combines distance, timing, and psychological factors, but you can't develop these through prearranged practices.

Aiuchi, which means to "strike at the same time," is a simple and effective way to improve the distancing and timing of your techniques. Just strike when your opponent strikes. To put it crudely, you don't need to defend. That said, your non-striking arm is defending your face. The easiest is to throw a jab or straight with your lead hand. This is because jabs and straights with your lead hand are the fastest attacks as your lead hand is closest to your opponent. Your fist takes the shortest route to your opponent. And because jabs and straights move straight from their initial positions to your opponent's face, they also block your opponent's line of attack and serve a defensive purpose. In Taikiken, striking over your opponent's line of attack is called Sashi-te.

We first throw an Aiuchi instead of blocking because blocking gives your opponent a chance to attack repeatedly with a second move, third move, and so on. When struck in the face barehanded, even a light hit to the eyes or nose causes tears to blur your vision. **Always attack back when you're attacked. It's a simple strategy.** When you do this, your opponent won't be able to attack carelessly.

As you continue to practice Aiuchi, you'll begin to sense the timing of your opponent's attacks through their eye, shoulder, and body movements. At first, as you get used to Aiuchi, you'll be reacting to your opponent's movements. But with practice, you'll begin striking first by reacting to the signs your opponent gives off when they're about to strike. Then, even when practicing Aiuchi, you'll be the only one striking. In time, your counterattacks will become preemptive attacks. But this doesn't mean choosing between a counterattack or a preemptive attack. It's just that when you're striking as your opponent strikes, your strike becomes a preemptive attack if your opponent doesn't strike.

Needless to say, you can't spend the entire bout with Aiuchi alone. Depending on how your opponent times their strikes, you may be unable to strike. When that happens, you can step back or put your guard up. **Simply take evasive action in the same manner (distance and timing) as you would throw an Aiuchi.**

There's also a mindset reason to base your strategy on Aiuchi. When defense is your primary focus, your mindset becomes defensive as well. While that alone would be fine, it can turn into fear. The right amount of fear is good because it leads to prudence and careful planning, but too much fear results in a contracted body, withdrawn posture, and your opponent sensing weakness.

Some may say that Aiuchi is reckless, as martial arts should be about self-defense. They are right. **Martial arts, in the first place, are about defending yourself against a stronger opponent.** There's no need to use martial arts against a weaker opponent. If that were the case, isn't it overly optimistic to assume you could endure everything a stronger attacker throws at you and escape unscathed? Of course, it would be ideal if you were unharmed, but isn't it more realistic to do whatever it takes to avoid a fatal damage, even if you're injured? This requires a mindset expressed by the Japanese proverb, "When drowning in rough waters, sacrificing yourself may be the only way to reach the surface."

Then, what about taking an aggressive approach instead of Aiuchi, assuming that a purely defensive approach will lead to defeat? When your opponent is in a vulnerable position and retreating, it is effective to move forward aggressively. However, you will get countered if your opponent is setting you up. While this is difficult to determine, if you observe your opponent carefully, you'll notice there are always **moments when they can't strike.** These moments will become clearer as you observe the moments when you can't move. No one can stay completely still. Your arms, for instance, are constantly moving slightly. And, while subtle, your arms will always have positions where they can and can't strike. By first carefully studying your own body, including the position of your gaze and center of gravity, you'll realize just how often you can't strike.

When being aggressive, it's crucial to gauge the openings when your opponent can't strike. Aiuchi may seem to contradict this approach, as you are striking when your opponent strikes. With Aiuchi, however, your opponent will find it difficult to take other actions. In other words, **when your opponent is striking, defending will be of secondary importance to them.** For this reason, you'll be able to land more shots than if you just charge forward on your own.

Let me to digress for a moment. While Aiuchi is a martial arts development, I find it intriguing how a similar game theory approach has proven effective through experiments. Game theory is the study of decision-making involving multiple parties with competing interests.

Within it, there's a thought experiment called the Prisoner's Dilemma. In it, a prosecutor offers the following deal to prisoners A and B, suspected of being involved in the same crime (A and B are held in separate rooms and can't talk).

- **Both prisoners are initially given five-year sentences. However, if they don't confess, their sentences will be reduced to two years due to insufficient evidence.**
- **If just one of them confesses, he'll go free, while the other prisoner will get ten years.**
- **If both prisoners confess, they keep their five-year sentences.**

In a deal like this, you'll only get two years in prison if you both don't confess, but if the other party confesses and you don't, you will spend ten years behind bars. Both of you would be free in two years if you both stayed silent, but if you only thought about yourself, it would be better to confess. What would you do?

Moreover, what would be the best strategy if you were to play this game repeatedly as one of the prisoners? To find out, political scientist Robert Axelrod held a tournament to gather various strategies and put them to the test. The result, going tit-for-tat proved to be the best strategy. In the first round, you should remain silent, but from the second round, you should do what the other person did to you in the previous round. If the other person confessed, you should confess. If they remained silent, you should remain silent. After this tit-for-tat strategy won the first tournament, it was pitted against more complex strategies in a second tournament. But once again, tit-for-tat came out on top. It was proven to be a simple but exceptionally effective strategy.

That was a lengthy digression, but it is the same when sparring. If your opponent attacks, always attack them back. Conversely, **if your opponent doesn't attack, don't attack them.** This then becomes a stare-down. This may not be the best strategy in a competition, where winning is the goal. But in self-defense or martial arts, where the goal is to protect yourself, this is one of the best strategies. Sparring is not a competition. A new perspective will emerge when you **break the unspoken rule to make "winning" your goal.**

Isn't a stare-down ideal in a real fight? Because both parties are uninjured.

Let me introduce how you can practice Aiuchi as just a reference. It doesn't involve directly attacking one another, so you'll be able to gain Aiuchi experience without any fear or worry of injury.

① **Face each other with your left feet forward (orthodox stance). Wear punch mitts on both your right hands and hold them directly beside your faces. We will assume that the mitts are your faces.** <Figure6-1>

② **Stand at a distance you would when sparring, and A will punch the other person's mitt.**

③ **B will then do an Aiuchi in response.** <Figure 6-2>

Punching distance means being able to step in to hit your opponent, not one where you can hit your opponent by just standing there. You'll

<Figure6-1>

<Figure6-2>

Face each other, hold punch mitts next to your faces, and punch right when the other person punches. Aiuchi is truly a fundamental yet ultimate strategy!

never spar at a distance where you can hit your opponent without having to move in. That's the distance at which you either knock out or are knocked out, and squaring up happens a step back from this. In reality, it's about another half a step behind this as there are kicks. Listen to the mitts to determine who struck first. As you repeat this exercise, you'll begin to sense when your partner is about to hit. There will then be times when B strikes ahead of A. While A is supposed to strike first in this exercise, this isn't a mistake. That's the right time for B to launch their attack. When A is hesitating whether or not to strike, that is precisely when B will be able to land their strike. That's because A can't move backward while deciding whether or not to move forward. Many Kenjutsu schools also emphasize Aiuchi as their fundamental and ultimate principle, albeit under different names, and studying it can provide many insights into sparring.

Defend and Attack the Center

Protecting your center while attacking your opponent's center is fundamental to sparring.

There are two reasons. First, it's because vulnerable points in the human body are concentrated along the midline. Even a light strike to an area such as between the brows, nose, philtrum (space between the nose and upper lip), throat, solar plexus, and groin would be effective. Second, it's because affecting something's center of gravity is an effective way to unbalance it.

When I say protecting your center, you might imagine, in a striking art, holding your hands up to guard your chin and centerline against strikes. While that's a part of it, "protecting" here means "maintaining." Maintaining your center doesn't simply mean protecting it from strikes; instead, it means maintaining your balance so that you can fully exert your power.

Your center, which is your midline, center of gravity, and awareness, is constantly changing. Simply put, your stance should mirror how your body would be oriented when pushing a stalled car. While the width of your center is too broad and ambiguous in this analogy, the idea is to refine it to a more precise sense of the center of your power. And because that center is always changing, it isn't simply about protecting your midline. Your strength increases toward your front, your centerline. If you crash into your opponent head-on while they are standing at an angle, you'd be able to overcome a slight weight difference. When you explore this phenomenon, you'll realize that even if two people appear to collide head-on, the person who more successfully attacks the other person's center can push with a greater force.

Imagine water flowing in a river. When encountering a rock, if it's big and heavy, the water will flow around it before meeting again. If the rock is small and light, the water would likely push it downstream. But the water doesn't think, "If the rock is big, let's avoid it; if it's small, let's sweep it away." It just hits every rock the same way.

Sure, it can be effective to strategize one way for a larger opponent and another way for a smaller opponent. On the other hand, you could approach every opponent the same way. But the movements will naturally differ even with the same approach. When you collide with a larger opponent, you are moved like water avoiding a large rock, and against a smaller opponent, you push through. Water just follows gravity and flows downstream. The weight of the water and differences in elevation create the flow. Maintain your center and attack your opponent's center. What we're doing is simple, but there is infinite change there. **We want to feel our weight and move accordingly, just like water.**

Strike Without Startling

Some people have a difficult time landing any strikes. While explosiveness and speed, or lack thereof, are big reasons why, there are other reasons. While there are numerous reasons, to sum it up, **that person's movements are easy for their opponents to react to.**

When you're gazing at a forest and a squirrel moves at the edge of your field of vision, you'll instantly notice that something has moved. **Our eyes are sensitive to movement.** You would see the squirrel even if the trees were swaying in the wind because its movement differs from those of the wind.

In this case, **movements are changes in contrast to those of the surroundings.** If the squirrel moved like the trees swaying in the wind, your eyes would miss it. When one thing moves differently from the others, it catches the eye.

Traffic accidents happen in intersections with excellent visibility, where a driver doesn't notice the car coming from the left or right. This happens even when cars coming from the left or right are visible from several hundred meters away.

While drivers do react to moving objects, when a car approaching from the side moves at the same speed as your car, the approaching vehicle looks motionless because the same angle between cars is maintained. That's when drivers overlook the approaching vehicle and accidents happen. **The car is in the field of vision, but it is invisible.**

<Figure 6-3>

We want to take full advantage of positionings where we temporarily disappear from the opponent's field of view, such as the spinning back fist and body shots where you step outside, but this requires a quick footwork.

We also want to use strikes that minimize your opponent's reaction while remaining in their field of vision. One effective way to do this is to **strike slowly.**

A reaction requires a reason to react. When sparring, people collectively sense the movements of shoulders, hips, fists, and even eyes as indications. And because you're constantly moving when sparring, your shoulders, hips, and fist are also in constant motion. They are the same as the trees swaying in the wind. A skilled fighter doesn't pay attention to every movement. They react to movements that differ in quality, like the darting squirrel.

Therefore, when striking, if you move without any triggers—any sharp movements—it will be difficult for your opponents to react. While I haven't measured the delay in reaction when doing this, it is very slight—probably less than a second. But this delay is enough to land a strike.

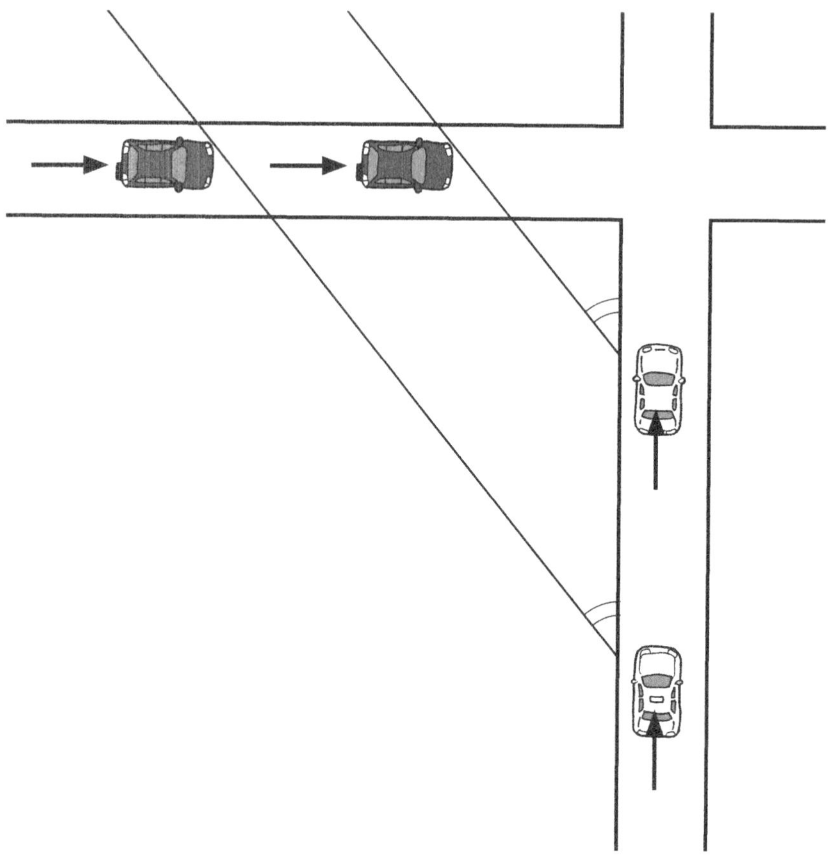

<Figure 6-3> Even if you can see the car coming from the side, it will appear motionless if the relative angle between it and your car remains the same. This can lead to accidents. In martial arts and sports, we also want to aim for movements that your opponents don't react to.

Striking slowly means moving without any sharpness to your movements. Instead of punching your opponent in the face, it's more like going to pluck a grain of rice stuck to their nose. Just do it in your everyday state of mind. If I were to give it a voice, it might be something like "Yup!" rather than "Bam!" or "Hi-Yah!" Your opponent senses and reacts to your attacking intent through movements in your shoulders, hips, eyes, and so on. **A skilled fighter reacts to the aura rather than to individual movements.**

So, if you punch without thinking, "I'm gonna punch you," you'll notice that your opponent's reaction is slower, even if you extend your arms more slowly.

A precise form is also crucial for such a strike. The ideal forms in any martial arts school should minimize movements that create unnecessary indications while maximizing power generation. Keeping your shoulders down, your head still, and aligning your body all also play a role in eliminating your indications. When you receive a boxer's jab, it looks as if only their fist gets bigger and bigger. It's tough to react as there's no unnecessary movement. **To swing at and to strike are two different things.**

As you get a feel for this, you'll be able to have both an explosive, blowgun-like strike, as well as one where you can change its speed and trajectory as you strike (like a homing missile) in your arsenal, so I encourage you to give this a try.

Acknowledgments

Master Michio Shimada, my teacher, has taught me many things. One of which is to "speak with your own words." Words that are parroted without any personal experience carry no weight or persuasiveness.

That's why I introduced the Rubber Ball Power in this book as a system called the Tripod Method. In martial arts, there are words like Peng Jin (spring-like power), Zheng Li (opposing forces), and Liu Mian Li (power in the up, down, forward, backward, left, and right directions) that our predecessors have left us. Still, I tried to avoid using them as much as possible. That is because no one can know if what you're experiencing is exactly the same as what those words represent.

The Rubber Ball Power learned through the Tripod Method is not a form or technique that is only useful for a specific sport or martial art. It is the power of balance that is inherent in everyone. In other words, it's a way to take full advantage of gravity. And when your body awakens to its innate balance, this balance will also transfer to your consciousness. Because it's something everyone possesses, by becoming aware of it, you'll be able to develop and apply it in any sport and everyday life.

The contents of this book are gifts from the guidance of many masters. In particular, I have composed this book based on what I have learned from Master Michio Shimada of Taiki Shisei Kenpo Kikou-kai, Master

Satoshi Amano of Taikikai, Master Hideo Kashimura of Chudokai, Master Seiji Sato of Kengaku Kenkyukai, Master Koyou Shigeo of Touzen, Master Mitsugu Yamamoto of Ryusuiken, Zen Monk "S," and many other teachers.

Finally, I would like to thank the many teachers who have guided me, the members of Buzenkai, my loved ones, everyone at BAB JAPAN CO., LTD., and you, the dear reader of this book, from the bottom of my heart.

Taikiken Buzen-kai
Ojiro Matsui